193

John Denver and Me

John Denver and Me

Jeannie St. Marie

Writers Club Press
San Jose New York Lincoln Shanghai

John Denver and Me

Writers Club Press
an imprint of iUniverse.com, Inc.

For information address:
iUniverse.com, Inc.
5220 S 16th, Ste. 200
Lincoln, NE 68512
www.iuniverse.com

ISBN: 0-595-14618-X

Printed in the United States of America

To my sister, Priscilla.

Contents

Some names have been changed. The rest is true.

Acknowledgements

For input, editing and support I am very grateful to Debi Cari, Louise, Carrie, Tina, Minda, and Bruce.

Introduction

If you go online and do a search for John Denver you will be amazed at what you find. There are over 400 websites devoted to John. (And over 40,000 web pages). Fan clubs abound. Every detail of his celebrated life and career can be found. The world loved John Denver and will continue to play his music for generations to come. And some fans may even seem to be a little obsessed about him. It's no surprise. John was one of the greatest recording artists of all time. This cherished singer/songwriter, musician, actor, and humanitarian contributed so much to the world of music and to the planet.

In fact, the Online Voters' Award for 1997 was given to John Denver—for Biography of the Year. While the Biography TV Show's producers did not select his life as the Biography of the Year ("Princess Diana" was aired instead), his online popularity prompted A&E to re-air his "John Denver Wildlife Concert."

One of my favorite www websites is: angelfire.com/folk/duncanpumpkin/archive—this website has a list of 51 tapes that its Webmaster is the proud owner of. In all, he has archived over 420 segments of John Denver including footage of interviews, concerts, TV shows, films, appearances, sporting events, the Olympics, and international telecasts. He will not part with any of them. Actually, I can understand why. Perhaps I became yet another obsessive fan, in my own way. If so, the obsession opened my heart and enhanced my life in too many ways to count.

Therefore, let's call it a passion for John Denver. He touched so many lives. I would venture to guess that one in ten people over the age of 30 has a John Denver story. A couple of years ago, a client of mine confessed she had gone to bed every night for a year with a John Denver album under her pillow. I'm sure I will continue to hear amazing stories about John Denver for years to come.

Chapter One—The Beginnings

It was the late Sixties. I was 17. My mother had recently passed away at the age of 47 and my father was dating. I was looking to escape. For me, the Woodstock era couldn't have happened at a better time. I attended Hammond High School in Alexandria, Virginia which is a suburb outside of Washington D.C. My friends and I would drive in to D.C. with our fake I.D.'s and go drinking at Old Ebbitt's Grill on 14th Street and see performers at various clubs in Georgetown. One night I saw a duo, Bill Danoff and Taffy Nivert, at the Cellar Door. I thought they were the cutest couple. They had actually met at a talent night there and went on to become Fat City.

Fat City became very popular—at least for a little while. Milton Okun produced their album, *Welcome to Fat City*, a Paramount Record; a short time later, Milt was to become John Denver's long-time producer. Back up singers on this popular Fat City album included a sister and brother, Susan and Chris Sarandon—who years later would become famous actors. Later, Fat City became The Starland Vocal Band ("Afternoon Delight"). Bill and Taffy Danoff wrote "Take Me Home, Country Roads" with John Denver. Soon after, John Denver would record that tune and it would become a huge hit.

Bill and Taffy also wrote and recorded "I Guess He'd Rather Be in Colorado" which is a song they wrote about John. They also wrote "Late Night Radio" which John recorded for his *Windsong* album; and Bill Danoff wrote "Baby You Look Good To Me Tonight," which appears on John's *Spirit* album.

At the Crew Follies (a talent show that raised funds for the high school's crew team that rowed the Potomac River) a then unknown group, The

Mamas and The Papas performed. Mama Cass had attended T.C. Williams High School and they were our sister/rival school. Film director David Lynch had just graduated from my high school—he used to design the sets for the school plays. The Beatles were leading the pack into a new rock and roll generation. It was an amazing time.

During the summer of 1968 I was a lifeguard at a posh high-rise apartment building that was next door to the Watergate Apartments. Hip and upwardly mobile young government and Capitol Hill employees lived there. Hit songs that I listened to on my transistor radio as I was perched on my life guard stand included "Mrs. Robinson", "Tighten Up", "Dock of the Bay", and "Born to be Wild". The other lifeguard, Kenny, became my first real boyfriend. He was older than me (by 5 years!) and was a wonderful artist who later went on to become an art professor at Virginia Commonwealth University. One night I eagerly relinquished my virginity on a blanket in a forest off the George Washington Memorial Parkway. The next day we were both covered with mosquito bites from head to toe. But it was worth it.

I don't remember exactly when it was I first heard John Denver on the radio but I remember thinking his song—"Take Me Home, Country Roads"—was the most exciting thing I'd ever heard. I became hooked on his music instantly.

In 1973, a two-and-a-half-hour made-for-TV movie, "Sunshine" aired on a major network. It was the true story of a very young woman who found she was dying of cancer and had kept a diary of her final days. The woman, played by actress Christina Raines, had a deep love for the music of John Denver, and requested that "Take Me Home, Country Roads" be played at her funeral. Another of her favorites was "Sunshine on My Shoulders," which lent itself to the movie's theme and title. The film also starred Cliff de Young.

The broadcast of "Sunshine" reached a wide audience, as did the eight Denver songs that were recorded on the soundtrack. RCA immediately reissued first a single of "Sunshine," then *Poems, Prayers & Promises*, the album on which "Take Me Home, Country Roads" and "Sunshine on My Shoulders" had first appeared. The album soon went platinum.

I remember the movie and the music vividly and I believe seeing it had something to do with my embracing the music of John Denver totally. His music had now begun to influence me already and he was now my number one favorite artist to listen to. His name, in a sense, had become associated with a celebration of life as well as a celebration of life—even in death. Perhaps a part of me resonated to his poignant sensitivity. Perhaps losing my mother at such an early age made the combination of the compelling story and his music so powerful. I cannot say for sure but I think this is when he began to hold a special place in my heart forever. My love affair with John Denver had begun.

I enrolled in The University of Tennessee in Knoxville and majored in Psychology and Drama. In the meantime, John Denver was beginning his extraordinary career. When I listened to "Rocky Mountain High," I wanted to go to the Rocky Mountains and see what he was talking about. He was the greatest travel agent on the planet. Over the years he would sing about Colorado—Aspen, in particular, and about China, Japan, Africa, Alaska, Montana, Australia, and Wyoming—yup, I made it to all of these places—eventually. He became a world citizen and sang about many other destinations as well. John found something inspiring, important or wonderful about every spot on Earth.

While at the University of Tennessee, I got very involved in the Vietnam anti-war movement and would have been arrested with the "Knoxville 44" if I hadn't left the rally early to get to a rehearsal at the campus Carousel Theater. My love affair with theater had begun in high school when I starred in "Bells Are Ringing" as Ella. My high school drama coach urged me to go to New York and pursue an acting career after high school but I was not ready and I wanted to get away from home and see what college was like. I had a blast. In college, I starred in "The Apple Tree" and "Fiddler on the Roof" and a number of other plays and musicals—I was making my mark on campus and this felt good since there were over 35,000 students at the college at the time. People would recognize me on the sidewalk and say what a great actress I was. It was a heady experience.

I guess you could say I was attractive. Maybe even beautiful at times. I was tall and thin and had very long, strawberry blonde hair and big blue eyes; I am certain I was prettier than I thought I was because I never seemed to have trouble attracting guys; the problem was I did not come equipped with high self-esteem. So I made up for it by doing things that would hopefully somehow prove that I was okay. In my last two years of college I lived with a law student, Richard. He was really a great guy and was a tremendous stabilizing influence in my life. Unfortunately, I was not ready to settle down at the time. (He is a successful happily married attorney in Chattanooga, Tennessee.)

At U.T. I remember seeing Janis Joplin in concert—she passed out half way through her performance—and the Ike and Tina Turner Review—I was in the front row—she (Tina) was—and is—the most amazing performer. I went to the Atlanta Pop Festival—which occurred a month or so after Woodstock—and I smoked grass, dropped some acid and had a wonderful time, except when our van broke down in a small Georgia town and the townspeople thought we were hippies (we were) and we thought we'd never make it out alive—we did. Life felt very exciting and dangerous. I was listening to The Beatles, The Doors, The Rolling Stones, and Pink Floyd but I was also listening intently to The Carpenters, The Association, The Fifth Dimension, and, of course, John Denver.

Chapter Two—Traveling the World

I was about to enter Graduate School in Ed. Psychology when I saw an ad in the newspaper hiring stewards and stewardesses for Pan Am. I had always wanted to be a stewardess. I didn't care what the intellects thought; this seemed like a dream job. Once again, I was encouraged by my friends and professors to go to New York with my drama classmates and pursue show business (since I was going to drop out of graduate school anyway) but I guess I wanted to travel the world more, so in 1973 I left Knoxville to begin training in Miami to be a stewardess—later that year all the airlines got together and decided we were all to be known as flight attendants—but this took years to catch on. My life changed dramatically overnight. After five weeks of training I was basking on a beach in Estoril Sol, Portugal within a matter of days. I joined a handpicked group of Pan Am Cabin Crew—we all spoke at least one other language—many spoke four or five languages and most of us were college graduates *and* the nicest bunch of people I've ever had the pleasure to work with.

Pan Am Training was fun for the most part. We learned a lot about dealing with emergencies and first aide and how to fold a napkin 100 different ways. The one thing I was not prepared for in training was the series of inoculations that would keep our arms sore and practically immovable the entire five weeks. I hated shots. If I had known there would be 16 of them, I'm not sure I would have shown up for training. Having all these inoculations to prepare for overseas travel certainly got me over my phobia about them.

Once I actually started flying, any illusions I had about the glamour of the business were very short-lived. On one of my first flights to San Juan, a fellow boarded the airplane looking ill. Before he had time to lurch into a lavatory he had projectile-vomited all over me, completely covering the front of my brand new uniform, my legs and leaving bite-sized chunks of god-knows-what on my patent leather in-flight pumps. I wanted to quit on the spot. But I hung in there even though I spent most of the flight in the lavatory scraping off the remnants. I had to laugh when a couple of flights later, we had a full load of crop pickers who had their roosters running up and down the aisle on our way to Haiti. Roosters and toddlers—the biggest problems to getting a cart down an aisle. I wasn't in Tennessee anymore, that's for sure.

I was based in Miami in the beginning and when we weren't flying it was party time. The best parties were the crew parties in exotic locales—with the flight attendants and sometimes the pilots getting together and drinking up a storm—lounging around swimming pools, restaurants, and discos in Rio De Janeiro, Madrid, Rome, San Juan, Guatemala, Buenos Aires, Panama, Barcelona, Lisbon and Rome. My world was filled with shopping, eating exotic foods, having overseas adventures, and of course, more shopping. Sometimes I would stop and think how incredibly lucky I was but eventually I took a lot of it for granted—the mind-set of the more "senior" crewmembers. We were, after all, for the most part "waitresses (and waiters) in the sky." But there was something special about being with Pan Am.

I had Paul McCartney on one of my flights—it was a 727—a very dinky airplane in comparison to what we have today—he was in First Class—of course—and we were flying from Miami to Barbados. He had a scotch and coke. It's funny what one remembers. Anyhow, he was very nice. Many, many celebrities were passengers on my flights over the years. A few years later when I was based in Los Angeles, I would fly a lot of "turn-arounds" from L.A. to New York. I was surprised if we *didn't* have some "special guest" on every flight. I watched Al Pacino rehearse his lines for "Scarface" next to a First Class lavatory and I helped John Travolta get tomato juice off his white suit. We used to fly Raymond

Burr, who was so nice and generous, to his private little island in the South Pacific. I thought that Gina Rowlands and John Cassavetes were the loveliest couple I'd ever met and Peter Lawford the strangest. The list of memorable celebrities goes on and on—but I think that book has already been written.

While in Miami I had my first overseas boyfriend. His name was Joaquin and he was a front desk clerk at our hotel in Portugal. He spoke very little English and the only thing I knew in Portuguese was "no fale Portuguese." He was very cute and very sweet and took me around to the private discos and restaurants of Estoril Sol. If the Presidential Suite was vacant when I checked in to the hotel on the many trips I took to Lisbon, Joaquin managed to arrange for me to occupy it. It was one of many fine perks of this romance. Both Joaquin and I knew in our heart of hearts that we weren't going to be together forever—our backgrounds were so very different. But I know we shared a real bond. We wrote each other for many years.

Flying was a lot different back in the 70's. For one thing, fewer passengers traveled. People actually dressed up to go on a plane. Most travelers were tourists, business people, or immigrants. For my first 8 years of flying, I never flew within the United States. And it seemed like most of our passengers were non-English speaking so I was able to pick up a little Japanese here, a little Italian there. Things went smoothly in the air for about seven months.

Then, on one flight from Miami to Managua, our 727 developed a little "mechanical" and the pilots were trained to land at the first available airport if the problem was serious enough. The nearest available airport was at El Salvador where Pan Am had recently suspended all flights because of a guerilla war going on. We had to land there anyway and when we got on the ground, armed militia escorted us to our hotel while the aircraft was being fixed.

It turned out we had to spend the night. The lobby of our hotel looked like a war zone. Men in army uniforms with rifles were everywhere. In the middle of the night, I heard a banging on the door next to mine. "Abrase, Abrase!" A loud voice was demanding that my next-door neighbor open his door. Then I heard a round of gunfire. I hid under my covers. The next morning all was quiet and as I left my room to go down to the lobby to wait for "pick up" back to our repaired aircraft, I noticed that bullet holes had riddled the door of the room next to mine. I looked forward to getting out of town.

After being in Miami for nine months I transferred to San Francisco. It seemed like everyone I met on the west coast skied, something I'd never done. For that matter, even though I had been through most of Europe and Central and South America, I'd never been west of the Mississippi. So being in California was a culture shock and it felt like a new world. But after only three months, I was informed that there were too many people at the base and that I either was going to be laid off or I had to transfer to Hawaii. I felt like I'd been given an E ticket to Disneyland. I loaded up my things and moved to the Islands.

Life as a Pan Am flight attendant in Hawaii was unreal. We even got paid more for being there! A typical schedule for me was to fly a two week trip from Honolulu—flying to Fiji and laying over for five days, then flying to Sydney and laying over for three days, then off to Bali for one day, and on to Hong Kong for three days, over to Delhi for two days, heading back through Bangkok for three days, then to Tokyo for a night or two and back to Honolulu. My plants were in desperate need of water upon my return but I would have up to two weeks off before I would do another trip. Sometimes I would do the "Around the World" trip, which would literally take us around the world on Flight 2—passing through Delhi, Istanbul, Rome, London, New York, San Francisco and then Honolulu. Going the other way, it was Flight 1.

In Fiji, it was a dream vacation. We could choose which island we wanted to stay on and a little boat would take us away for five days. My favorite island was Castaway. They had luscious buffets all day long and we stayed in little huts on the beach with ceiling fans blowing in the ocean air. We would swim and ski and snorkel. Whatever we wanted to do. After five days in the sun, it seemed a shame to have to get back on the 747 to continue the journey to Sydney, Australia but you do what you have to do. We Hawaii-based Pan Am flight attendants wore puka shells around our necks and at night on the plane we would kick off our high heels (I can't believe we wore high heels on the plane back then!) and walked around in slipper socks. We were a radical bunch. And they had hired a bunch of male flight attendants so there were a lot of couples flying together. Everyone seemed to be getting married except me. Settling down wasn't exactly something I was hankering to do although I had my share of some interesting romances.

There was one particular pilot who was infamous in the airline. He name was Perry Medallion, and he was known as "Perry Medallion, the Golden Stallion." He was blonde, tan, young, and really handsome. (Most Pan Am pilots didn't look like Perry, believe me). Perry had his Pan Am pilot uniform tailored in Hong Kong. No one ever said exactly *why* he was called the Golden Stallion but just use your imagination. I flew with this famous pilot one night on our way to Pago Pago, a remote Polynesian destination I loved. It was still quite primitive at that time and there was only one hotel on the whole island—The Rainmaker.

Well, one thing led to another and I wound up with Perry after I'd slipped and fallen on the concrete in the rain during a raucous middle-of-the-night pool party. He bandaged my knee and stayed with me for the rest of the layover. From then on, I would have interludes with Perry who'd be sitting waiting in the various hotel lobbies around the world when he would look me up and see me on an in-coming crew list. It was very exciting.

I flew to many, many places. Some places I flew to and got to know quite well. My favorites were Hong Kong, Tokyo, Bangkok, Singapore, Rome, Samoa, Seoul (best shopping in the world) Fiji, Auckland, Sydney, Buenos Aires, Rio de Janeiro, and Athens. My least favorites were Barbados, San Juan, Tehran, and London. I really don't know why. I *loved*

India. Going to India was like *really* going to a foreign country. It was incredibly primitive at the time—maybe it still is. Cows wandered everywhere. People would just go to the bathroom by the side of the road. If a cow wanted to come in the front door for dinner, no one was going to kick her out. I rode an elephant around the grounds of my hotel and dined on exotic tandoori cuisine. The shopping was the best. But most of all, the energy of India was comforting. I always felt very safe there. (The energy of the Hawaiian Islands—and for the most part, all the South Pacific—is also very comforting—like you are held in the arms of God.)

Back then—who knows what it's like now—people in Australia and New Zealand, could not do enough to help you out. If you had a question or needed to get somewhere, it was nothing for an Australian or New Zealander to literally drop what they were doing, maybe even take the rest of the day off from work, and show you around town. Parts of Europe were like that as well. 9 to 5'ing it is definitely an American-made thing. And, of course, in Latin and South America and parts of the Orient, all shops are closed from about 2-4PM while everyone takes a nap! What a concept!

Tehran was so weird. They always gave the males on the crew their rooms first at the hotel. I had to sit in the "women only" section of the hotel coffee shop. If I wanted to go shopping, I had to cover my whole body—no bare arms or legs showing—and we always had to travel in pairs. I did bring back some great caviar, however.

My in-flight experiences had exciting, scary, or memorable moments as well. I flew for Pan Am for 13 years and in that time I only had one safety-related incident. Shortly after a take-off from Osaka, Japan in around 1982, there was a loud bang and the plane started to shake. We had "lost" an engine. Now what that *usually* means in airline lingo is that the engine stops working. In this case, we had actually *lost* an engine—or at least a very large part of it—it had fallen off the plane! We all looked out the left side windows—"we" meaning the flight attendants and the passengers—and something was very missing from the wing. The passengers were amazingly calm. Maybe when you can actually see a problem it isn't as bad as if you imagine a problem. Anyway, we had to dump fuel immediately and make a near-emergency landing back in Osaka. The pilots didn't make too much of it. They liked to brag about the 747 and how it could fly with only one engine. I was never very interested in seeing that actually happen.

On another flight we were sitting on the ground in Nassau with a 747 planeload of passengers. The plane needed some kind of last minute repair and all of the pilots and the ground mechanics were outside of the plane, looking perplexed, staring up at an engine. (Does not bode well for confidence.) It must have been over 100 degrees in the cabin. We were away from the gate and they wouldn't let anyone off the plane. There was no food since it was a short run and the beverages were almost gone. The passengers got restless, then they got angry, and finally they began to riot and run all over the plane, stealing all of the liquor out of the carts. One passenger threatened to throw me out of one of the back door exits, which we had opened to let air into the cabin. This was one time in my career where I abandoned my position and hid in the cockpit until things blew over.

For the most part, at least in "those days," passengers behaved themselves and we, as flight attendants, were always nice. We were paid to be nice, no matter what. Times have changed, haven't they? Two babies were born on my flights—both right before landing, and I had one passenger, er, die on us—not our fault. We had a lot of people pass out on the long haul flights and I had a passenger *bite* another passenger—he insisted he was a dog and even bit the ground agent when we landed. And I caught all the pilots asleep in the cockpit just once. "Coffee, anyone?" I asked nonchalantly.

Back in the early 80's, I had a man in First Class offer me one of his lines of cocaine he had carefully etched on his tray table. (There was a time when a lot of partying went on up in First Class). One airline even had a piano lounge. Those days are way over. Other than seeing the Northern Lights from 30,000 feet, the most incredible thing was to land in Hong

Kong. They have a new airport now so you can't get the thrill we used to. Shortly before touchdown in Hong Kong the planes would fly through a narrow corridor completely surrounded by high-rise apartment buildings. On either side of the plane you were so close to the buildings you could see—and actually wave at—the people in their homes. You could see people cooking food, hanging laundry, and taking a shower—all the while traveling by their windows and balconies at about 300 MPH in a gigantic aircraft. It was the most amazing sight to see. As far as I know, there was never an airline crash in Hong Kong—thank heavens!

There was a period in the 80's when we flew hundreds of Vietnamese orphans, accompanied by American Red Cross volunteers, into the United States. Many of these children and babies had problems associated with malnutrition, infections, and neglect. It was heart breaking to see. But it also felt good to know that our country and our people were taking in these innocent victims and that they would be in loving homes soon.

While I was living in Hawaii I got an urge to act again and I starred in a local production of "Company"; I also got small parts in "Hawaii Five-O" and a "Charlie's Angels" episode when it taped in the Islands. I got my SAG card when I landed a part in "Pearl Harbor"—a TV mini-series starring Dennis Weaver, Robert Wagner, Angie Dickinson and Leslie Anne Warren. To this day, I still get residuals from this job—although it's a tiny amount. I was feeling pretty good about myself as an actress. I started doing commercials and was chosen the Queen of St. Patrick's Day and floated (well, sat on top of the back seat of a Cadillac convertible) down Kalakaua Blvd. wearing a flowing green dress and waving to the crowds.

I had to find out what this skiing thing was all about and so I went to Aspen for the first time in 1974—I chose Aspen because that's where John Denver lived. I never thought I'd run into him on the slopes but he had made Aspen sound so great in his interviews and in his songs. It was even better than I thought. There is definitely something to that Rocky Mountain High—actually, I think it has something to do with the lack of oxygen at that altitude—I was instantly high as soon as I landed at Aspen Airport.

I took five days of ski lessons at the Aspen Highlands with a bunch of other airline employees—we got a real deal in the prices. I don't believe I've ever had so much fun. We stayed at the Roaring Fork Condominiums. I loved it so much I went back whenever I had a break between flights. One winter I actually managed to live in Aspen most of the time, after hooking up with a ski instructor. We lived in a trailer just outside of town. I thought all ski instructors were gorgeous—it turned out that it was just the tan face and the cool outfits. Underneath, they are all very pale.

Back in Hawaii, I lived in a house with three other flight attendants—on the water in Hawaii Kai. I had a ski boat which I spent a lot of time repairing. But we skied, played tennis, and partied. I loved the ocean and I got my scuba divers certificate. I don't remember if John Denver had recorded "Calypso" at the time but when I listened to this beautiful song about the sea and Jacques Cousteau—the most famous ocean explorer of all time—and his ship, the *Calypso*, it always brought me back to the joy of being in the ocean.

While in Hawaii I tried surfing, sailing and even spinnaker flying. Spinnaker flying has you flying on a rope behind a sailboat without much control—in my case, I slipped and flew out of the swing at such a high altitude that when I landed in the water I broke a tooth. I was much better at water skiing.

I had a friend who was a jumpmaster and he took me skydiving. I was very scared but, clearly, I was an adventurer at this time in my life. I wanted to try everything! We went to Dillingham field on the North Shore of Oahu. I took a 4-hour course and learned how to survive in case I landed in the water or somewhere other than the drop zone. But Mike, my instructor, insisted that it was very safe and that learning all this survival stuff was routine. We climbed aboard a small plane and took off. At about 5000 feet one by one we jumped out of the airplane. I have never been so scared in all my life. I was all alone standing on the wing and Mike yelled, *Jump.* So I jumped. I think I went unconscious for a few seconds. But soon my shoot opened automatically—I was on a static line, thank God—and I began to float down to earth.

I had a little speaker attached to the front of my equipment where I could hear instructions but they could not hear me. Mike was telling me which toggle to pull. He kept saying, *Pull the left toggle*, then a few moments later, *Pull the left toggle.* I kept pulling the darn left toggle but for some reason I began to drift away from the landing zone and out to sea. There was silence and I was getting closer to the ground. Finally, Mike said, *Prepare for a tree landing.* What?!! Okay, I had to think back to the training and knew instantly to cross my arms and legs and lower my head. Seconds later, I landed in some trees, some very tall trees, yards from power lines and a few more yards from the Pacific Ocean. I couldn't believe this had happened! I also couldn't believe I was alive. What a rush! I was hanging in midair amongst the trees and ever so slowly I managed to get myself wrapped around a trunk of one tree and I just held on tight. It took them over two hours to get me out. The next day I flew off to Aspen and skied the best I had ever skied—all the black runs on Aspen Mountain. I was fearless, at least for a few days.

While in Hawaii, I heard about this thing called EST. and that it changed peoples' lives. So I took the EST training and found it quite mind-altering. I worked in the EST office for a while after taking a ton of their follow-up seminars—About Money, About Time, About Sex, and so forth. I read that John Denver took EST a short time after in Aspen. I thought it was neat. A number of his tunes were clearly shaped from his Werner Erhard experience including "Looking for Space," "Love is Everywhere" and "Farewell Andromeda (Welcome to My Morning)." I thought it was a great thing, this EST; the training was about taking responsibility for your own actions, being on time, and telling the truth faster. Unfortunately, some of the best concepts of this 70's phenomenon didn't permeate the bulk of society. At least in L.A., no one is *ever* on time!!

I made two life-long friends who I met in the EST training. One was my friend Bob. Bob was this tall Japanese American bundle of enthusiasm for life. Bob and the other friend I made, Merikay, hung around like the Three Musketeers. At the time, Bob was living in a small apartment and working as a sales rep for Xerox. We all belonged to the same softball team. Bob also played an intense game of rugby. Merikay and I would go to these rugby games and cheer the Hawaiian team on. Teams from other countries would travel to Hawaii and play this rough-and-tumble game with the Hawaiian team. Bob introduced me to a really cute Aussie player. His name was Peter and he became my *Australian* boyfriend for about a year. And every time I'd fly to Sydney we'd go out and have a wonderful time.

Bob married a friend of mine, a fellow Pan Am flight attendant—I went to the wedding—but it was a short-lived marriage. Janet, the bride, wanted Bob to stay with Xerox to provide some security. Bob had other ideas. I recall he had BIG ideas back then. He loved the idea of becoming an entrepreneur; he was so enthusiastic about everything, it was mesmerizing. He gave me this little Velcro pouch that I could lace onto my tennis shoe so I could stash a key in there. What a clever idea. He loved Velcro stuff. I lost touch with Bob after I left the Islands. But, some twenty years later I found him again. He was on the Oprah Winfrey show! "Bob" is now known as Robert Kiyosaki, best selling author of *Rich Dad/Poor Dad* and a multi-millionaire. Wow, Bob! I had dinner with him and his lovely wife when he passed through L.A. I was fortunate to be able to sit in on his lecture, which had been sold out for weeks. It was great. And Bob is—er, Robert—is the same guy I always knew—and a whole lot richer!

I continued to keep updated on my favorite recording artist, John Denver. I knew that he was married to a lovely woman named Annie and he wrote so many beautiful songs for and about her. I figured that even though he also wrote about the problems, it was a love that was more than I could even imagine. I thought she was so lucky to have John. And then when they adopted their children, Zachary and Anna Kate, I knew they had created a wonderful family and I could only admire that. I never thought that this wonderful being—John Denver—could ever be in my life. So I stayed a distant fan but never strayed from his music for long.

A year or so after I took EST, I took another training, The Loving Relationships Training, which had been created by Sondra Ray. It was wonderful. Towards the end of the weekend seminar, Sondra said to the group that the most important thing we could do for our lives and our destinies was to get rebirthed. (This was in the mid-70's) I had no idea what she was talking about but it intrigued me.

Rebirthing had been discovered by Leonard Orr shortly before that and people were getting amazing experiences and results from the process. So I hopped on board and got involved with rebirthing, and to this day I am closely connected.

I met Leonard Orr a year or so after that. He had just come back from India where he had been staying at an ashram in Herakhan with Babaji, the Immortal Maha Avatar. There seemed to be a lot of yogis available at that time—Rajneesh, Muktananda, Maharishi, etc. but Babaji never left His India and apparently had been coming back in human form for some 10,000 years. This time around He stayed from 1973-1984, having materialized His body in a cave. Sounds incredible but there was no one disputing this fact. So when I met Leonard he had just been with this Babaji for a month. Just being with Leonard for a few minutes made me higher than I'd ever been—a "contact" high. I felt enormous waves of love and clarity, I didn't need to sleep as much, and I could even drive my car with my eyes closed. (Not recommended unless you've been with Babaji)

Babaji had thousands of devotees but only a few Americans had "discovered" Him. The people who traveled into the jungle to find Him were Indians and Europeans mostly. The rock band, Supertramp, stumbled upon Babaji and was never quite the same after. They wrote a song about their experience with Babaji, which is on one of their top-selling albums in the 70's, *Even in the Quietest Moments*. When you fall into the energy of

Babaji—whom many consider to be God in human form—it envelopes you with total love and bliss, heals your karma at breakneck speed and changes your life forever. He left his body on Valentines Day, 1984.

I felt very connected to Babaji and loved by Him, even though I hadn't visited Him in Herakhan. In the months before He left His body, which of course I didn't know He was going to do, I felt that Babaji was making things happen in my life. I felt so empowered by the love of Babaji I had the thought that He was somehow responsible for having my wildest dreams come true. I remember wanting $10,000 and a few days later I won $8,000 on a game show. Close enough, I thought. Then I wanted to meet Steve Martin who had just done a show in Hawaii—when he was doing his balloon act and his Egyptian routine—sounds weird now but it was a hilarious performance. Anyhow, sure enough, Steve showed up the same week on one of my flights. He was with Bernadette Peters and they were both wearing white. They sat in 4E and F. They were a lovely couple. I overheard Steve telling Bernadette he thought I was pretty. I remember blushing and feeling very acknowledged. I would never have imagined what what going to happen very soon in my life and I've always wondered if the awesome Being of Babaji had something to do with it.

Chapter Three—Flying Solo

After five years of being blessed by the loving energy of the Hawaiian Gods and Kahunas I decided it was time to make my move and pursue my acting career in Los Angeles. Besides, I don't think there was any one left in Hawaii for me to date—all the good ones had been taken or so it seemed. Leaving Hawaii was one of the most difficult things I've ever done. It was gut-wrenchingly painful—but I knew I had a destiny to discover. I arrived in L.A. in July of 1978—I went to someone's 4th of July party and I was freezing.

I was a long way from Honolulu. I had a tough time adjusting to Los Angeles. I naively assumed that I would get an agent and begin my meteoric rise to acting fame. I really wanted to be a star of a sitcom. I knew I was very funny and comedy was my favorite thing to do. I wanted to have the kind of role that Julia Louise Dreyfuss epitomized ten years later in Seinfeld. Goofy, smart, and outrageous. I didn't know that about 100,000 other actress hopefuls had come to L.A. the same year with the same idea. All the joy and love and spontaneity of my performing got lost in the sea of new self-doubts, extraordinary competition, pictures, resumes, ego-squashing acting "classes," criticism, bad experiences, and just plain struggle. And I was one of the lucky ones. I still had a great job with the airlines that I could escape to when the rejection got too hard.

Things did not go well in my acting career for a long time and lord knows I tried everything. I did plays, I wrote my own scenes and performed in showcases sometimes three times a week, I did stand-up comedy, I took a million acting classes—cold reading, improvisational comedy, commercials, you name it.

I actually won a talent competition for my stand-up comedy but, truthfully, it wasn't something I was that excited about; it was meant to be a vehicle for my career. My act revolved around a New Age kind of lifestyle I was into. "I took so many seminars, I put name badges on my pets...I asked my gas station attendant if he had anything he'd like to share...I took so many seminars I found I had no time left so I took a seminar called "Stop Wasting Time"—it lasted a year...You know you have cellulite when you're sitting in your yoga class and your leg has spread out like pizza across the floor"...and so on. I did have my funny moments and I enjoyed the writing process.

I must have spent $5,000 on pictures and resumes, postcards, stationary and video demo reels in less than a year. I got agents, I lost agents, got a manager and when my manager left the business, I tried submitting for jobs on my own. It was pathetic. Things were not happening and I was getting older by the second —but I would take classes on mind control, and centering and creating the job happening and chanting for the job to happen, and spiritually cleansing so that I could approach the acting with renewed vigor and a positive attitude (no matter how much I'd been dumped on). I had convinced myself that I was destined to be an actress, a paid actress, and nothing was going to stop me. I had a destiny, a gift, something special to offer the world.

Unfortunately, those 100,000 actresses I mentioned before—they also were convinced of the same thing. I remember sitting outside many a casting office waiting to audition and looking around the room. Somehow they had found 15 other women who looked exactly like me—and some even had the same mannerisms! It was mind-boggling. It never crossed my mind that a few others maybe shared my "something special."

Occasionally I would audition for something and the response would be wonderful. I was told that I had terrific comedic timing and could be a big star with all my different characters. On other occasions, a teacher or casting person would say to me after I had poured my heart and soul into an audition piece, *What the hell do you think you are doing?* Or, I would simply be dismissed while some other wunderkind got all the praise. You have got to be nuts to keep at it like I did. But I was nuts. I got so nuts that I purposely pulled myself away from acting for a while to try and "find myself again."

For a while, I sang in a trio with two other ladies. We called ourselves "The Redheads." We wore big, red wigs and slinky dresses and sang harmonies of songs from the 50's, 60's and 70's. "Put Your Head on My Shoulder," "From Russia With Love," "Then Came You," "Both Sides Now," were some of the tunes we re-visited. Audiences seemed to love us but we broke up after a year or so due to some "creative differences." One of the singers remains a good friend of mine and has gone on to be quite successful singing with big bands and with her new husband, a well-known singer and musician.

At this point, I *really* took a departure from show business. I began flying lessons. I knew it would help my self-confidence and—among other things—stretch my brain a little. My dad is a pilot—retired—and lives in a fly-in community in Florida where everyone has a house and a hanger—with one or more planes—and the backyard is a taxiway. He builds planes and is an in-demand guy in the neighborhood, helping everyone build their planes. He is an expert at what he does. My dad is also a retired NASA engineer. John Travolta has a home and more than a couple of planes housed in the community. It is a very special place. Lots of working and retired airline pilots live there as well—never getting too far away from the world of aviation. I had been in one of my dad's planes a few times and it seemed like a very cool thing to do.

Learning how to fly was scary for me; I learned early on that I was not a "natural" pilot. My knees shook when I took off; in the back of my mind was the thought that I was counting on that one engine to get me up and if it failed a really nasty crash was inevitable. I enjoyed landing a lot though. I was also terrible at navigation. When you are driving a car, you can always look at a map at a stop light to see where you are going or if you're really lost you can pull over and really study a map—or even ask someone for directions (last resort—this rarely works anymore for some reason). When you are flying, you can't pull over and look at a map; you can't even *look* at a map for very long because your eyes need to be on the conditions outside and on your instruments.

After I started to solo, I got lost constantly. I even landed at the wrong airport once. It had the same runway numbers of the airport I was trying to find but when I got on the ground, I found that it was an abandoned airstrip with a bunch of chickens roaming around. (At least I was able to stop my plane, eat a sandwich, and read my map before I took off again). It was lonely up there too—I decided that any ideas I had about becoming an airline pilot were forgotten. (Quite a few former flight attendants learn to fly, rack up the flying hours and become airline pilots.) I think I would have felt confined in that cockpit. I liked moving around, socializing with people.

I finally got my pilot's license but shortly after I did, my flight instructor got hired as a pilot for a cargo airline on the East Coast. On one of his first flights he hit some bad weather and crashed his plane and was killed. Someone from the FAA called to tell me what had happened. I was stunned. I couldn't believe that he was gone.

A short time after that, I had a "near-miss". Actually, what had happened was that I was planning a take-off from an airport in Santa Barbara. I had radioed for the weather down in Torrance—where I had rented the plane. This is a standard procedure to check the weather at your destination. Everything was clear. So I took off around 3PM and headed south. I was just about to enter the Los Angeles International Corridor—which is a space above Los Angeles International Airport (LAX) that small planes can cross over—flying perpendicular to the runways—at certain altitudes.

Suddenly, a marine layer moved in. A marine layer is like fog. It's fast and it's dense—and it shows up sometimes in the late afternoon along California coasts. This was a weather condition I had not heretofore encountered while flying. I had very little training in instrument reading and I was depending on my outside visibility, which was quickly turning into zero. I looked below and could barely discern big jets below preparing for take-offs or landings on LAX's runways and taxiways. I knew I had 12 minutes more before I was over Torrance Airport but I couldn't see.

My instinct was to panic but when you are alone in a plane, panic is not an option. So I prayed like I had never prayed before. I shifted into a robotic kind of mode, and counted the 12 minutes before I knew I'd be over the airport. I radioed in. I could not see below the marine layer. So I brought my altitude down even more. The tower was helping me out somewhat but I was relying entirely on my instruments. It seemed like a miracle but there was a section of the layer that was thinner than the rest and I could vaguely make out some runway lights. I kept saying to myself, "I'm going to make it. I'm going to make it." But I had no idea how.

I began my descent and approach. I was the only aircraft trying to make a landing so I was cleared to land. I began to see more as I got lower but it was eerie and objects seemed distorted. I made one approach but I came in too high and had to go around. I imagined that I would be going around all night. I tried a second time and was again too high—although I was getting more accustomed to the conditions. On my third try, I made it with a bit of a thump. I was drenched in sweat but I was ecstatic. I had made it! But it had been close.

It took me a while, but I got back to my flying—both with Pan Am and in the little Cessna 152 I piloted myself. As it turned out, I began to date the fellow from the FAA, who had given me the bad news about my former flight instructor, and we flew a lot together in a twin engine Piper that he owned. It felt better to have another pilot on board.

Any of the men that I dated and got close enough to me would discover that I had a "thing" for John Denver. I had every one of his albums and had begun my cassette tape collection. I had a scrapbook with articles I had saved from the newspaper about John. I never dated anyone for long that didn't like John Denver.

It always amazed me how shut down people were about him. Some people actually couldn't *stand* John Denver, many of them music critics. In my opinion, John was on the planet to lighten it up and open peoples' hearts. I think his quest alone—seen as a kind of 70's Don Quixote— threatened some folks, especially macho guys.

In response to the critics, John observed, "When you're a positive person there are people who would like to find something sordid or crummy about you and I just refuse to be anything other than what I am." A critic from the New York Times once wrote, "What bothers me most about Denver's music is that it's so boring…a corny sentimentality that just doesn't register on any deep level." Let's just say it didn't register with *her*. Some people just didn't get it and as John Denver probably would have said, "That's fine. Not everyone's going to get my music."

In the face of many critics' onslaughts over the years—accused of being saccharine, bland, mediocre, boring, banal, monotonous, and corny—John was quoted as saying in his own defense regarding one particular critic. "The guy said he couldn't find any relevance in my music. You know why? Because his life is probably a drag. He can't tell if it's sunny outside or raining because of the smog. If he wants his life to be a drag, it's all right to me. Critics don't mean a thing to me. When I'm raising a family and enjoying life in the mountains on a full-time basis, they won't matter then, either."

He did admit later, in a *Rolling Stone* interview, "I sometimes get upset by reviews. I think it's one of my weaknesses, one of the things I haven't quite gotten through yet…People who would review a concert and out of 18,000 people one guy would write a review, and I know that 17,999 people were at a different concert than that guy was at—but, see, that's the concert that he was at. I resent it or used to resent it and maybe I still do. This is one of the things I need to get through, that people, quite often critics and reviewers, editorialize as opposed to review…If they just said, now this is how I felt as opposed to this is the way it was, because I feel that I've gotten some of the worst reviews of concerts and albums that I've read."

I regularly—at times, daily, would play John's music simply *to feel*—feel happy, feel sad, feel excited, feel hopeful. And certainly if I was feeling one way when I would listen to a John Denver tune I would feel entirely different when the song was over—usually lighter, inspired or moved. I *required* his music like some people require church for peace of mind. And, I cried a lot.

But even crying over a broken heart, or a missed opportunity—when accompanied by John Denver—was a beautiful thing. I learned some of my favorite songs—"Back Home Again", "Take Me Home, Country Roads, "Leaving on a Jet Plane", "Looking For Space" and "Rocky Mountain High"—and would practice singing in my car while I was driving to an audition or stuck in L.A. traffic.

I had never seen John Denver in person (yet) or at a concert but I had seen him on television. When I saw the film "Oh God" in 1977 starring John Denver and George Burns, and saw John up there on the big screen, my heart stopped. I *loved* him. I loved the movie and saw it a number of times. John was the biggest performer of the 70's decade. The whole world was discovering this enormous talent and humanitarian. And even if some people thought he was corny, his trade mark greeting, "Far Out," became a household expression and heralded in a period of progress, discovery and spiritual enlightenment.

If someone had asked me who I wanted to be stranded with—on a desert island -my immediate answer would have been John Denver. Or if I only had a month to live, who would I want to meet—same answer. He truly made a difference in my life, and of course, in millions of peoples' lives. Who knows how many people got married to "Annie's Song"? It must have been hundreds of thousands. In the 80's he wrote a tune, "For You"—another love song so perfect for a wedding—which should have been a big hit but, unfortunately, the music industry had moved on to other artists.

John could have written the greatest song of his life in the 80's and it wouldn't have gotten airplay. That's just the way it was. Ironically, artists from the 70's are now making a big comeback but John isn't here to participate which I know he would have loved. It must be difficult for anyone to be so on top and to begin any kind of descent. I heard Kenny Rogers say recently, "You (any hit recording star) only have three years and the rest is downhill. It's just getting used to that downhill."

Though his star had faded in recent years, John Denver seemed in the last year of his life to be undergoing a Santana-like transformation from seeming obscurity to a kind of celebrity re-incarnation.

Chapter Four—John and Me

Although I had gotten *some* work as an actress it wasn't much for all my efforts and I decided that I should try "growing up" and think about doing something else with my life. I have learned since never to do anything if the only thing that is making me take action is thinking I *should*. At least for me, it never, *ever* works out. " I *should* love this guy because he loves me. I *should* take this awful job because it'll be good for me. I *should* keep my appointment even though I'm sick as a dog." Wrong!

I picked up a book by Gerald Jampolski some time after this "should thing" was happening for me—*Good-Bye to Guilt—Releasing Fear Through Forgiveness*. Wouldn't you know John Denver wrote the Foreword! (Hmm…had he struggled with the same thing?) John wrote, "In the recent 'Me Decade' there were myriad programs, training centers, workshops, and seminars, which allowed us to focus on ourselves as individuals, and to use self-awareness and self-expression as tools for self-help and the expansion of consciousness. For many, myself included, it was also a step toward spiritual growth and understanding. What was rarely, if ever, included in the descriptions, analyses, and criticisms of the 'Me Decade' was its possible impact on the world we live in and its potential for affecting society as a whole.

Many of us have wished that the world were different and wondered aloud about how we could change it and make it a better place for everyone to live in. I am one who believes that we cannot change the world, but that we can only change ourselves, and in the process, the world will be different. I truly believe that we can create a new and better world....I know that the thousands all over the world who love Jerry [Gerald G. Jampolsky, M.D.] and whose lives have been enhanced by his message are eagerly looking forward to his new book. They have a treat in store. In clear and beautiful prose Jerry tells us that peace is a conscious choice. Saying good-bye to guilt is a vital step in making that choice."

Gerald Jamplosky is also the best selling author of *Love is Letting Go of Fear* and a number of other noteworthy books. He and his wife, Diane, were close friends of John's and they were present at the October 1997 memorial service in Aspen. They had brought John's ashes from California.

Getting back to my trying a grown-up kind of thing, I got this job opportunity where I would sell tax-sheltered annuities to school teachers and non-profit companies. The plan was that I would make a whole bunch of money, be in a grown-up career and leave Pan Am. Sounds exciting—not! At the time, Pan Am was giving six-month leaves of absence (they were trying to reduce the employee ranks as all the airlines were struggling financially). It was perfect. I would take the six-month leave, do the tax-sheltered thing, and return to flying if it didn't work out.

My last trip before my leave of absence began was a seven-day Los Angeles to Sydney to Honolulu to Los Angeles trip. The first leg was a late night departure non-stop from L.A. to Sydney—took about sixteen hours. I'd done the trip a million times. This night—in January 1983—I was thrilled to get the usually very "senior" position of First Class Cabin Attendant. It was a lot of work up there in First Class—we served three meals, had two movies and had an all-night buffet—but traditionally on this flight people slept a lot.

I was counting the meals when Tim, the flight attendant I was working with, told me we only had four passengers in First Class—yay!—But to be sure we had a vegetarian meal on board for John Denver. I froze. I will never be able to adequately describe the host of feelings, thoughts and emotions I had in that moment. I numbly said to Tim, "Who? Who has a vegetarian meal?" Tim seemed distracted. "Uh, John Denver," he said. "*The* John Denver?" Tim looked at me strangely. I had to ask myself, "Is there another John Denver in the world—am I going insane?" I knew in my heart it was John. Beyond a shadow of a doubt. John Denver is about to walk on board this plane? Oh my god, oh my god, oh my god. I ventured out to the cabin but my knees were wobbly, my mouth was dry. Before I could get a chance to regroup myself for this momentous occasion, a few seconds later John himself walked on board. He looked around the cabin, gave me a big BIG smile and I almost had a heart attack.

It was the most amazing smile I'd ever seen. I was beside myself. I couldn't speak, much less go out and serve him a pre-take-off beverage. I slipped into a lavatory—fell is more like it—and looked at my face in the mirror. I looked like I was on some kind of acid trip. Something was happening to me and I didn't know what it was. I was scared, happy, crazy, and high and my heart was beating wildly. (Babaji, what have you done to me?) I attempted to calm myself down and pretend like everything was fine—I was, after all, an actress—but I fear I didn't do a great job.

In no time, John had asked one of the other flight attendants who came up from the economy section to "check him out", if *I* was okay. I managed to babble a few things and get the meal served. I was putting things away when John got out of his seat, walked into the galley and said, "Hi." I was on the floor, sliding trays into carriers, and I looked up and said something that resembled a "Hi" back. I stood up and we stared at each other a few seconds. He seemed very tall—actually, he *was* tall—much taller than I thought—perhaps about 6'1"—and he was looking very handsome. He was very upbeat and energetic.

He asked me if he could go upstairs. I said sure, did he want anything? "Yes," he said. "Would you go up with me?" Oh, God. Now, the upstairs of our 747SP was an additional section of First Class seats but it was completely empty on this flight. And the cockpit is upstairs, of course. So John and I went upstairs—I needed to check on the cockpit anyway. So as I went in to the cockpit, John hovered around outside. The Captain immediately asked him to come in so John was hanging out in the cockpit with the pilots and engineer and was just one of the guys. The cockpit crew loved having him come and visit—and they talked airplane talk for a while. (Of course, it is now a big FAA violation to let anyone in the cockpit during flight). After we exited to the upper cabin, John asked me to sit down with him for a while. This was one of the greatest moments of my life. But then there were more and they kept getting better.

John and I sat in two First Class sleeperette seats (this is a seat with a foot rest and that leans back and makes for a comfy bed on long flights) and we talked for several hours. I never wanted to get up from that seat for the rest of my life. We had a wonderful conversation. He was more interested in hearing what I had to say about things than to talk about himself. It blew my mind. We talked about being from military families (he was Air Force, I was Navy). We talked about flying airplanes. He loved hearing about my dad's airplanes. We talked about seeing the movie, "Gandhi," and how we both had cried at the end. He told me he was inspired to write the song, "It's About Time," after seeing the film. He told me that he was separated from Annie and that they were getting divorced. (Actually, he didn't need to tell me that since I'd been following the whole saga word for word in the media).

I found some extra pairs of blue Pan Am slipper socks and for fun we both took off our shoes and we sat there with our feet stretched out in our matching blue slipper socks. We giggled like kids over doing this. It felt very natural to just "hang" with John like this. I don't believe I ever curled up with another passenger in quite the same way. Off in a darkened corner of a 747SP. All alone. We were settling in to our private section of the airplane and no one knew where we were. Maybe everyone else was asleep or didn't really care. It was womb-like.

I felt so happy just sitting there with him; yet, I was having a major out-of-body experience as my biggest dream in the whole wide world was happening. How can I adequately describe how this whole thing felt? I can't. But I was filled with a feeling of love, bliss and joy; it was indescribable. He was so excited about an upcoming possibility that he would be the first civilian in space. (This information was to become public sometime after this). "I've been working on this for a long time and I think it actually may happen," he told me. A few years later, in 1986, when school teacher Christa McAuliffe was part of the ill-fated Challenger crew, John wrote a beautiful song—"Flying For Me"—to honor their memories, knowing that he had longed to be a part of this crew.

I told him my favorite John Denver song was "Looking For Space." "Why?" he asked. "Because," I said, paraphrasing his lyrics, "sometimes I fly like an eagle and sometimes I'm deep in despair." He was impressed! But then, of course, he wanted to know what difficult times I may have been though in my life. I tried to think of one. Frankly, just sitting and talking to John was vindicating every bad experience I had ever had. I was in love and more in the moment than I'd ever been—who cares what happened yesterday?

John was impressed that I was a pilot. But I didn't hide the fact from him that I was not that great at it. He didn't mind. I shared with him my wild airplane experiences. We laughed a lot. We also talked about silly things. Like our favorite foods, our favorite places. He would alternate between being serious and being witty. He was very attentive. And focused. It was not easy to put one past him. He told me that something weird had happened shortly before the flight regarding Bob Hope. I guess Bob had insisted John come over to his (Bob's) waiting jet to visit. John didn't see the point. But he felt somehow obligated and obliged the renowned comedian. He clearly didn't like being manipulated. As it turned out, John was to become a yearly guest at the Bob Hope Celebrity Gold Classic. (A few years later John began to host his own annual Pro-Am Celebrity Golf Tournament in Tucson every January.)

John shared with me that he had lost his father in March of the previous year and was still feeling the loss. "You know he taught me how to fly." he said. "I know," I replied. I told him I had lost my mother when I was a teenager and that I was sorry to hear about his dad. "It's been a tough year," he added. We were silent for a bit. Then we talked a little more about our parents and what an impact it has when they leave us.

But I was also officially on duty and this little voice would interrupt my thinking from time to time and say, "Uh, Jeannie, maybe you should look in on the cockpit—it was my job, after all, to feed "the cockpit" (the name used to describe the pilots sitting in the cockpit at the time—could be up to five of them) and look in on the other three First Class passengers from time to time. But, as it turned out, the other Flight Attendants "understood" what "my job" was turning out to be on this particular flight and they didn't give me a hard time about disappearing for hours.

Eventually, as the morning light over the Pacific Ocean started to peek into the windows, I knew I had to get up and prepare for some kind of service. "I've got to get back to work," I said finally. He smiled and looked me squarely in the eye. "I understand," he said. So, we got up and we went downstairs and John went to sleep (lucky guy) and I went to work. During our entire visit, John never seemed to get tired; he appeared to be always very "present."

I felt good. I didn't feel "complete" but I felt good. I had just spent hours with my all-time biggest idol and this alone was the highlight of my life. Could there be anything greater than this? (I have met a lot of stars, even dated a few celebrities, but this was the whole enchilada, the big Kahuna, the million-dollar jackpot, this was my baby, John Denver!) Two of the other First Class passengers, as I recall, were accompanying John to Sydney on his tour. They included his road manager, Sam, as well as another key associate, Ron. I hadn't slept at all on the flight and I was getting breakfast ready—we were about an hour and a half out of Sydney.

It just so happened I had brought my camera on this trip. I told the other flight attendant working with me, Tim, that I would love to have my picture taken with John to capture this wonderful experience. Tim encouraged me to dig out my camera from my bag. Tim was enjoying the whole unfolding drama between John and me. We had been buddies for years. God rest his soul, Tim died from AIDS only a few months later—this was in the beginning of the AIDS crisis. No one at the time really knew what it was much less have a treatment for the disease.

Anyhow, wouldn't you know as I'm on my hands and knees once again on the galley floor, John walks in to see what we were up to. I had to grab this opportunity. I got up from my stacks of trays and asked John if he wouldn't mind if he had his picture taken with me. He seemed to be very happy to do so. So Tim took a couple of pictures of us standing there behind the last row of first class seats next to the galley. John just naturally put his arm snugly around my waist. Whew! So I returned the gesture. It was a memorable moment.

John went back to his seat so I could serve breakfast to him and his companions. I felt, momentarily, that having this picture taken would be the final chapter. But I had a nagging thought—a screaming thought in my head, actually, that I *must* see John again. I told Tim. Tim smiled and said, "Why not?" But I threw it out of my mind as I began to prepare the cabin for landing.

Then he was there again, John, standing there before me by the galley. We were descending, a few minutes from landing. He looked mildly uncomfortable as he stood there. I was almost tempted to suggest he get back to his seat and fasten his seat belt for landing but I thought the better of it. Finally, he said what he had come to say, "Would you like to go out this evening?" No one was standing behind me so I knew he was talking to me but I wanted to look behind me to see for sure. I was so stunned I just stared at him for a few seconds. I said yes. He gave me this big John Denver smile and I melted. He said he would call me after we all got to our respective hotels. Well, I was in a zombie-like state for the next two hours or so. Landing, luggage, customs, crew bus to our hotel at King's Cross. And sure enough, he called me shortly after I floated into my hotel room and we set up our date.

Chapter Five—Weekend in Sydney

I was so excited but I was also a wreck. I hadn't slept on the flight and I certainly wasn't able to sleep in the few hours before I would see him again. He called again and asked me if it would be okay if Sam and Ron came with us, accompanied by two other flight attendants. It turned out that the two other flight attendants had become friendly with these two other guys and had made arrangements to get together. They all thought it would be fun to go out in a group. It didn't matter to me—in fact, it made it a little easier. I liked the other two girls who came along. One was a good friend, and the other I had known since Pan Am Training School. I spent the time waiting, figuring out what to wear and wandering around in an altered state.

At the appointed time we showed up at John's hotel downtown Sydney in the lobby bar. Right on schedule, "the boys" walked up to our table and sat down. It was clear who was with whom. It felt so great to see him again and he was in wonderful spirits. We began an evening I will never forget. It just flowed. It didn't hurt that Sam and Ron had made all the arrangements. We walked down to the Sydney Harbor and arrived at an elegant Chinese Restaurant overlooking the Sydney Opera House. We were greeted at the front door by a staff that treated our group like we were royalty. We had the best table and the best service you can imagine. And the six of us had a grand time.

At the time, John was a huge star in Australia—much bigger than he was in the States—he was a god. His concerts on the following evenings had been sold out for months. Our little party attracted a lot of attention at the restaurant. It got a little crazy when at one point, a woman lost control and rushed over to John, grabbed him and kissed him while her husband was trying to pull her off. After that, the waiters made sure people couldn't get too near the table. I was amazed at how nice John was through the whole incident. We spent a lot of time laughing—and drinking—and eating great food and watching the sun set over the harbor. It was a dream. We told jokes—airline jokes, all kinds of funny stories. John remarked that he thought I was funny which made me feel great.

It was clear John, Sam and Ron were very close friends. My girl friends were having a blast. In the middle of dinner, John said, "Let's have a toast." For a moment, no one knew what to say. Then, my girlfriend Debi lifted her glass and said, "To Poems, Prayers and Promises." It was a wonderful moment. John was obviously touched. And so we all lifted our glasses to toast over one of John's most beautiful songs. Our group suddenly felt like we'd been friends forever.

A girl came up to our table with a basket of roses. John bought me a rose that I still have today, squished into a photo album commemorating that trip. It got late and we got up to leave. Sam wanted to settle the bill but the owner came up to our table and told us that we didn't have to pay because it was his honor to have us there. I couldn't believe it! The restaurant was filled that night because word had gotten out that John Denver was there but it was still an awesome thing to behold. As we exited the restaurant, there was a crowd of paparazzi waiting outside. John signed a few autographs and took it all in stride. Flashbulbs were popping everywhere but before I knew it we were whisked into a cab (that Sam I'm sure arranged magically as he always did) and back to their hotel. John asked us all up to his penthouse suite for after-dinner drinks.

He had a huge, lovely suite but what made it amazing was that every square inch was covered with bouquets of flowers and baskets of fruit from friends and fans. One whole wall had been set up by RCA, his record label, with extensive stereo and sound equipment for John's use. We sat in leather couches and drank Grand Marnier. John put on some music he liked—*Autumn*, by George Winston. And we sat around and talked. John was a wonderful storyteller—you could listen to him for hours. Then, John stood up and asked us if we'd like to listen to the master of his soon-to-be-released newest album, *It's About Time*. I was thrilled. So he put it on.

I was sitting there about to hear some of John's music that I had not heard before and John was sitting next to me possibly waiting for my reaction. Instead John stretched out on the couch and put his head in my lap. I can't begin to tell you how I felt when he did this. I had died and gone to John Denver heaven. *It's About Time* is a beautiful album, definitely one of his best. John told us how much he enjoyed recording "Wild Montana Skies" with Emmy Lou Harris—the song is one of the most exciting and memorable on the album. But it also has some very sad songs; songs he wrote while breaking up with Annie. (This album is not as sad as *Seasons of the Heart*, which was his current release at the time). I have always cried when I listened to John Denver's heart-touching songs and this was no exception. Side Two starts out with "Falling Out of Love" which is followed by "I Remember Romance"—that's the one that sent me over the edge. A few of my teardrops landed on John's shirt and I hoped he didn't see. Thank God it was dark in the room. It was very silent in the room while we listened to this beautiful album.

When it was finished there was an awkward moment. Something was happening between John and myself and it didn't involve the others. Suddenly everyone was getting up and quietly excusing himself or herself and talking about getting together the following evening for the concert. And just as suddenly John and I were alone. My heart was pounding. John then asked me, "Would you stay?" There was never any doubt. I nodded. He took my hand and led me to the bedroom.

He kissed me and we held each other for a long, long time. He began to unbutton my blouse and I began to unbutton his shirt. How many times have I seen this in a movie? And then we just finished undressing ourselves. He was standing there in just his underwear. He was wearing plain white BVD's. I remember thinking, "Oh that's interesting—he's not wearing boxer shorts or colorful jockey briefs, he's wearing Fruit-of-the-Loom!" He also had no hair on his chest and seemed to have a nice even tan all over his body — he looked fantastic without clothes on. I was hoping I did too.

We threw ourselves onto his bed and began making love. He told me he I had a beautiful derriere. (Actually I think his exact words were, "You have a *great* ass.") I figured a big pop star like John Denver would be more of a receiver than a giver. But I was wrong. To top everything off about this man, he was a wonderful lover. I hadn't had a lover like John in years. He was giving and caring and tender. He loved—how shall I put this—kissing every part of me…It hurt to be so well taken care of. How could he be this wonderful? Doesn't he know I have to go back to my humdrum life after this? (Or do I?) I think we went to sleep for a few hours and then we made love again. Later we were lying on our sides and he was holding me from behind. "What are you thinking about?" he asked me. I didn't know what to say. I didn't know what I was thinking. I didn't think he would want to hear that I never wanted to leave him; that I had never been happier in my life. What would he think? "How nice this is," was my reply. Duh. We drifted back to sleep.

Morning arrived as it has a way of doing. John was up before me and the first thing I saw was John putting on jogging clothes. He smiled and said, "Jeannie, please stay—I'm just going running—I'll be back." I couldn't believe he had the energy to go for a run; I could barely move. He gave me an embroidered denim shirt—a trademark John Denver shirt to wear while he was gone. I wandered around his suite wearing his shirt. I read some of the cards attached to his flowers. So many loving admirers.

There was a knock on the door. It was room service. The deliverer wasn't sure who I was but I signed for the delivery. It was a wonderful breakfast for two and I hoped that John would get back in time to have some of it. I had some coffee and a croissant and took a shower. This woke me up somewhat.

Eventually, John came back and told me he had run ten miles. Wow! We sat and talked. It was then that John noticed a small florescent green spot on his shirt that I was wearing. He got upset and asked me how it got on there. Actually, I had no idea. It didn't even look like it came from Earth. It glowed. I told him I didn't know and that I was sorry if I had done it but I didn't have a clue as to how it got there. Was he planning to wear this very shirt tonight on stage? I felt bad. But he dropped the subject as suddenly as he had brought it up. We ate some of the breakfast and, yes, we went back to bed. It was glorious. This time it was slow and gentle. He stroked me lovingly. "I love your neck," he said. "I love your everything," I wanted to say.

I knew at some point I had to go back to my hotel and get ready for the concert—and maybe even get some sleep. But John had an interview to do so he was up, took a quick shower and was dressed in no time. We held each other and then he was off. Before he left he told me to make sure to connect with his manager about coming to the concert that night. He wanted me to stay until he got back but I told him I should probably get back to my hotel and change clothes. That was fine with him. He looked forward to seeing me later. And he was out the door. I never thought that it would be the last time I would see him for almost two years.

Chapter Six—Afterglow

When I got back to my hotel I was horrified to find that Pan Am had rerouted me to return to Honolulu that very evening. I was so conflicted. I, of course, wanted to see John again but there was no way I could get out of this change in itinerary. I felt horrible. After much consternation, I went back to John's room. I knocked on his door but there was no answer. So I slipped a note under the door saying what had happened and sadly went back to my hotel and got ready to fly to Honolulu.

As it turned out, John was extremely upset that I had gone. His managers told my girlfriend who was lucky enough to see his concert that night that John was devastated by my departure. If he only knew! If I had to do it over again, I would have called in sick for that trip and stayed to be with him but I simply didn't have the sense to do it at the time. When I got home to L.A. two days later I called John in Sydney. They put me through right away. John's mother had arrived and he was happy about that. We talked for a while and then I never heard from him again. But you don't have a thing like this happen without some kind of fallout. I felt like a changed person. Actually, I was a changed person.

For one thing, John had been so complimentary to me as a woman and as a person, I was not sure I would ever be able to be with another man who didn't totally adore me. (I managed, unfortunately, to stumble upon another one or two over the ensuing years before I moved on to better relationships).

But, most importantly, being with John did something to my spirit—it inspired me in some way. John lived life totally—he seemed to face life, love, feelings, problems, sadness, new experiences, world issues—*everything*—head on. He seemed to live like we were all meant to live—with freedom—even if there was fear, loss, embarrassment or pain. This is what I have aspired to ever since. I knew I had to live and not just survive like I had been doing. I sold those tax-sheltered annuities for a few months but it didn't feel right. I realized I had to follow my dream once again—what was life for anyway? My connection with John had affected me at a cellular level.

So, once again I tried jump-starting my acting career. This time it didn't work out so badly. I started to do some commercials and got some great corporate gigs that sent me off to places like Orlando, Washington D.C., Vancouver, and New York to do videos. I also got a recurring role on "Days of Our Lives" and another recurring role on "L.A. Law"—I played a reporter. Granted, my dialogue amounted to lines like, "Mr. Sifuentes, what did you think of the jury's verdict?" But it was show biz and the money was great. On "Days," I was an ob/gyn (Dr. Ruth Levitt) and was limited to saying things like, "Jennifer, congratulations, you are two centimeters dilated."

While things began to happen for me as an actress, I also worked as an entertainment publicist. I figured this was a good way to get "inside" the business. As an actress, I only felt like an "insider" when I had an acting job. As a publicist, I handled some interesting celebrity clients and hung out backstage at The Grammy's, The Peoples' Choice Awards, Comic Relief, and the CMA's. I also attended a number of other star-studded events.

On one particular "Star on the Walk of Fame" ceremony, I was there for Lorne Greene, star of the television show "Bonanza." He was Canadian so many of his fellow Canadian actors were present at the Brown Derby celebrating with the celebrity after he has been awarded his star on Hollywood Boulevard. Impersonator Rich Little (and a Canadian) seemed to take a liking to me. He was very charming, witty and handsome and we chatted for some time—flirted might be a better word. (I looked him up in People Magazine archives later and found out that he was married). He pursued me somewhat afterwards, wanting to whisk me off to Las Vegas on a private plane, all expenses paid. Hmm…I wonder what he had in mind? It was tempting but to tell you the truth, I wasn't interested. First, he was married. And second, he wasn't John Denver.

The head of the PR firm I worked for was absolutely crazy. A frenzied maniac who ran around the office saying, "I don't have time, I don't have time!" At least he wasn't mean-spirited like some could be. I was amazed that, years later, after I had left the PR business, he had become John's publicist! I also found out that someone I had gone to high school with was John's publicist in Aspen. (There must be something to that six degrees of separation theory).

After a while, though, I returned full time to acting. What I discovered about the entertainment industry wasn't pretty. If you had a bad childhood and would like to re-create the experience as an adult, just get a job in show business. It is the *most* dysfunctional business on the planet. Of course there are a few pockets of good people and good projects and great talent but the land mines are hard to miss.

I had one job for more than a year selling syndicated television shows for a major distributor. The president of the company was a psychotic madman. My boss, a dear man, was fired for no apparent reason. I worked my ass off while I watched a $125,000-a-year "vice-president" sit in his office all day reading the trades. I got a new boss who was afraid of losing his job and sold me down the river to protect himself. Our 18-year-old beautiful blonde receptionist was regularly hit-on by the middle-aged guys at the firm—I sat near the coffee lounge and saw her awkwardly trying to get out of their clutches. I had about enough when we needed to move our offices down the hall to another suite. Suddenly, all of the "men" claimed to have back problems and us "gals" had to pack and move all the boxes ourselves. I don't *think* so! The company was too cheap to hire movers. That's when I got back into full-time acting.

Eventually, I got a big, starring role in a nighttime episodic—it was great to be getting work but for some reason it didn't make me any happier. In fact, I didn't really enjoy these experiences as much as I thought I would. I would be given my own trailer with a television and phone. And I'd spend hours in another trailer—"Make-up and Hair"—being primped to the max and then outfitted with an $800 wardrobe. But I was still coming home to my one bedroom apartment in North Hollywood. After all of my years of chasing the carrot of show business, getting the work wasn't making me as happy as I thought it would. If only the part had been bigger, if only I was younger, if only I could get a steady acting job, if only I could get a good script, if only, if only…

I took a seminar with an entertainment consultant, Breck Costin. The room was filled and everyone was excited. He was known for "busting" people. He busted me. "Either get 100% behind your career or get out of the business," he used to say to a roomful of aspiring actors and writers. I was wondering what had happened to my commitment. I felt lost. He had been an actor at one time and had some pretty good roles but had given it up to do what he *really* wanted, which was to lead seminars and follow a path of "absolute freedom" and to let go of attachment to results. A whole new world opened up for me by exploring this path.

After over 20 years of pursuing an acting career, I found myself giving it all up to have a life. In truth, I was sick of running all over town in some new outfit with my hair and make-up perfect to try to get acting jobs. I hated sitting in casting offices because I invariably compared myself to the other talent in the room. I felt free when I gave it up. I have never looked back. I was in love, anyway, and in a long-term relationship with an attorney. I was also beginning to make a living as a rebirther and with conducting seminars of my own.

I had a girlfriend who desperately wanted to meet John Denver. So, one night we drove down to Irvine Meadows Amphitheater to see a John Denver concert. It was around 1986. I had never seen a live John Denver concert after all that had transpired. He was so fantastic, words can hardly describe.

Harold Thau, John's business manager for many years, put it beautifully in the Introduction to John's Autobiography, *"Take Me Home"*—written in

1994. "Moments before the house lights dimmed, the Coliseum manager breathlessly informed me that eighteen thousand people were here—a new house record had been set. The audience is, as always, composed of both men and women, some old, some young, many in their thirties, forties, and fifties, all roaring their approval as the announcer booms through the darkness, 'Ladies and gentlemen, John Denver!' And then John's voice soars above the din, soothing us and unifying us with his masterful songs, many paeans to the joys of a natural world. We listen and allow ourselves to respond; we become part of his poetry. There he is, one man holding thousands of people with the clear, pure sound of his music. Even after so many years, I am still overwhelmed by the power of his artistry."

I hadn't seen John or talked to him in two years. But as luck would have it, we got to go backstage because Ron, who'd been on the Sydney trip, recognized me and let us in. While we were ushered through, I was amazed to pass a seemingly normal looking fellow who had turned into an obsessed fan being hauled away by security, all the while kicking and screaming and demanding to see John Denver. Amazing.

"Backstage" is actually two things. There's the backstage—a crowd of media, people from the record label, special guests, etc. And then there's *backstage*. We were allowed in to this inner circle—the real backstage. It was us and the musicians from the show and the crew. It was an incredible experience to see all of the equipment and human labor involved in his concert. It was mind-boggling. There was a trailer—for guests, I guess—where there was a lavish buffet with all kinds of food, which no one was eating. Everyone was waiting for John to show up from somewhere. And there he was. Looking wonderful. He recognized me immediately, which surprised me. I felt a little funny because I was in this relationship and had "moved on", so to speak, in my life. But "it" was still there for me. I was struck again at how genuine John was. His sincerity and earnestness were real and intoxicating. I introduced him to my girlfriend Mimi.

I was to find out years later that John had not only remembered me the night I came backstage but had cherished that weekend in Sydney with

me. Apparently, he would periodically ask a mutual friend about me—
What was I doing? How was I? But he never *acted* on his curiosity by getting in touch with me. I always figured he was too busy (he was always
busy) or had found a new girlfriend—which of course he had.

Mimi later managed to get a lunch with him at the Bistro Garden in
Beverly Hills but it took a lot of pursuing on her part. I had no intention
of trying to "start something up" with him again. I knew, even then, that I
was emotionally incapable of being in his world for very long. Mimi said
her lunch with John was very emotional. He seemed to be very sad, she
said. At the next table was Dorothy Hamill and they talked with her for a
while. Later, Mimi met up with him again in Aspen at a conference but
they never connected after that. And neither did I.

But he was always in my heart. Somehow, I knew everything would be
okay as long as he was somewhere. It didn't matter that I didn't see him or
speak to him for years. So when he unexpectedly died, I was sadder than I
ever thought I could be; a part of me had been counting on him always to
be here on the planet. Who could ever be what John was for the world?
Who sings for the planet now? And, for me personally, and for those who
loved him, the loss of his presence on this plane—to uplift our spirits, to
enlighten us, to move us to help those in need—is overwhelming.

While backstage he announced that he was boarding his airplane in a
few minutes and flying to Monterey. His back-up singer, a pretty lady was
hitching a ride with him. He wanted to know if we wanted to join him. I
guess it was kind of out of the question but something to ponder about
later. I was jealous of his back-up singer—and all back-up singers at that
point. They seem to have such great jobs. I wondered if he'd ever slept
with one of his back-up singers. I knew John had been around. Women
adored him.

After my famous Pan Am flight, word had circulated a bit and I was
always being filled in someone's John Denver story, either real or imagined. One flight attendant I met said she was on *the* camping trip with
John and Annie and her own boyfriend when John wrote "Poems, Prayers

and Promises." Now *that* was impressive. Another crewmember told me about her friend whom John had pursued but she had turned him down because she was in love with a Pan Am pilot. (It must have been Perry Medallion—who else could it have been to turn down John?). I know John also dated a few celebrities, a list which included Susan Anton, Shirlee Fonda and Cheryl Tiegs.

I don't believe John was every truly happy again in a relationship after Annie. Close friends say he may never really have gotten over the breakup of his marriage even though the two had come a long way in healing their relationship. In 1988 he married Cassandra Delaney and he became a father again when baby daughter, Jesse Belle, was born in May of 1989. The marriage lasted a short time. John was very devoted to Zachary, Anna Kate, and Jesse Belle. The three biggest joys in his life were his children, flying and singing. His closest friends will confirm that.

John's closest friends and associates were not necessarily the same people who he had to deal with for his career. He talks about this in his autobiography. There was one particular concert producer who was not a very nice man to put it mildly. Right before John was to go onstage to do a concert in Honolulu in 1983, this "friend" told John that his soon-to-be ex-wife Annie was vacationing in Maui with her new boyfriend. This news upset John so much that he almost cancelled his show that night. On a lighter note, John had one of his managers send some flowers and a card saying something intimate to a young lady he had just spent the night with; the flowers and card were accidentally sent to her parents.

Other major artists, including Neil Diamond, were always trying to steal John's musicians away from him but they were intensely loyal to John. They also had a great time touring with him—the quality of the music and the camaraderie was always there. A number of John's musicians had come from amazing backgrounds. His guitarist, James Burton, had been in Elvis Presley's band (as well as with Roy Orbison, George Harrison and Elvis Costello) and saxophonist Jim Horn had been with the Stones and the Beatles.

Even though I was in my relationship, I secretly followed John's career every step of the way. I was so impressed with his music as it evolved. He recorded awesome songs in the 80's and 90's. His involvement with world hunger and environmental issues became an even bigger mission on his part.

And how can you describe a voice like John's? As you listen to his recordings and his live performances in the years after he was at his most popular, it is incredible how his voice *got better*. There is a performance I will never forget. It was a televised special for Jacques Cousteau's 75th birthday. John performed live, just himself and his guitar and sang "Calypso." It was a heart stopping performance and his voice hit the notes like never before. It was electrifying and the audience went crazy.

It's been almost three years since John left us—seventeen years since we first met—and about ten years since I last saw him in person. For about six years during the 90's, I stopped listening to his music. I stopped because I felt in some way it was keeping me in the past and not allowing me to move forward in my life. But I never stopped loving his music and I never stopped loving him. On many occasions over the years I have been shopping at Ralph's or sitting in a hotel lobby or, yes, even standing in an elevator, and a John Denver song will be playing in the background. I find myself listening and having all kinds of feelings. Mostly I feel happy and alive. Sometimes I feel a little sad. And sometimes I just feel.

I fell in love about six years ago with a man I knew just a little about. We moved in together quickly. It wasn't long before I discovered the new love of my life was a musician who wrote beautiful songs. (I thought he was just a plain old sound mixer). He was an amazing natural talent—he was self-taught and played piano, guitar, bass, drums as well as sang and composed music and lyrics—*and* he was good!

He had been the drummer in a popular 70's band on the East Coast, which had disbanded before ever getting quite rich and famous. He was just getting back on his feet having struggled with a substance abuse problem. In the years I was with him he wrote some great songs. I wrote the lyrics for a few of these songs, which we got published and sung by recording artists. We put a CD together which still sells on the internet. His songs had the same spirit that John's had in many ways. He wrote the most beautiful songs for me. We also wrote together one of the *best* Christmas songs.

But the perfect mixture of qualities that distinguish out a talent like John Denver is not available to everyone and even though my lover was hugely talented, major success so far had eluded him. My partner also had a dark side. (Do *all* talented musicians have dark sides?) The dark side was very dark. I can only imagine what kind of dark side accompanied John Denver on his human journey. And my empathy goes to those closest to him—his family in particular. It is not easy to "be" with someone's darkness. It became impossible for me to "lighten" up the darkness in my relationship but I was committed to my partner and I was good at "weathering" bad times.

It didn't seem to matter—my relationship suddenly ended last year anyway. It was a real setback in my life. I am much better now and we have remained friends. But, at long last, I pulled out my John Denver music again for some solace and inspiration. Wow. I cried. Wouldn't you know the magic is still there! It was like no time had passed. His sound is just as uplifting and awe-inspiring as it always was. And I am so happy to be listening again—perhaps I will never put the music away. And, in any case, why should I—or anyone for that matter?

This is the music that sets me free, opens my heart, and gives me the optimism, courage and possibility that my dreams can always come true. His life and his art contributed more to the world than he ever knew. His message was universal, his voice incomparable and his music was—and is—magic.

Chapter Seven—John Denver Biography

This is a John Denver abbreviated unofficial biography. There are many official biographies of John Denver and I encourage you to seek them out. John Denver was born Henry John Deutschendorf, Jr. on December 31, 1943 in Roswell, New Mexico. His father—an officer and test pilot in the Air Force—and his mother, Erma, were very young parents. Five years after John, his younger brother, Ron Deutschendorf, was born. Being a military family, they moved a lot. By the time John was 16 he had lived in Japan, Alabama, Arizona, Oklahoma, and Texas.

A shy boy, John learned to play the guitar at an early age, a mostly self-taught discipline he spent hours in his room perfecting. He began to play folk songs in high school—in vogue at the time. He enrolled at Texas Tech in 1961 to study architecture (to please his parents) but dropped out and moved to Los Angeles to pursue his music dreams.

In 1964 when he started to use his stage name John Denver (took "Denver" because it was more record-label friendly and because he liked the Rocky Mountains) he was a regular at Ledbetter's in Los Angeles. In 1965, he got his first big break when he replaced Chad Mitchell in the Chad Mitchell Trio, a pop-folk group that toured the college hootenanny circuit of the 1960's. He was with the Trio, now known as Denver, Boise & Johnson, for two years.

It was on this circuit that John met the love of his life, Ann Martel, in St. Peter, Minneapolis in the spring of 1966. After an on and off again courtship, they were married in June of 1967. The Trio broke up in November of 1968 and John and Annie moved to Chicago.

Not much happened until John was hired to perform as a solo artist at the Leather Jug in Aspen, Colorado. He was very well received in Aspen and he wrote his first song about Colorado, "Aspenglow" in 1969. "I'd had a lot of beautiful experiences there. The whole stay had given me a tremendous lift when I badly needed one. The local people were so involved in that friendly way of life, and when I finally sat down to think about it, I wrote the song in about fifteen minutes. I tried to capture something in the spirit of the people there and the way they treated me. The friendliest people in the world, I think, are skiers."

Shortly thereafter, he was given a chance to perform at The Cellar Door in Washington, D.C. with friends Bill and Taffy Danoff. John had already written "Leaving, On a Jet Plane" (in 1966) but it didn't find fame until Peter, Paul and Mary recorded it as a single in 1969. It became a smash hit and their first No. 1 song as well. As the writer of a hit song, John's career began to gain momentum.

Bill was writing a song that he was struggling with and after a show one night, Bill and John stayed up all night and finished "Take Me Home, Country Roads." They recorded it in New York and it went on John's *Poems, Prayers and Promises* album. "Country Roads" was released as a single in the spring of 1971 but it started slowly. RCA was about to pull the plug on it but John insisted they work the song a little more which they did. And on August 18, 1971, it became a certified million-seller, his first of more than 40 pop hits.

Within two years, John dominated the Pop Charts with "Rocky Mountain High," "Sunshine On My Shoulders", "Annie's Song", "Back Home Again", "Thank God I'm a Country Boy", "Calypso", and more. He had suddenly become one of the top stars of the decade. It was an extraordinarily prolific period for John Denver. John and Annie were able to move to the Rocky Mountains that they had dreamed about. After "Country Roads" hit in 1971, the Denvers erected their dream home in the beautiful Starwood area of Aspen, Colorado.

John reached a commercial peak in the mid-1970. His *Greatest Hits* album, released in 1973, stayed in the Top 200 for more than three years and sold more than 10 million copies. He had 14 gold albums (selling at least ½ million copies each) and 8 platinum albums (for sales of more than a million copies). He had many gold and platinum sales overseas as well, including Australia, Germany and the United Kingdom. By 1975 he was the biggest selling recording artist in the world.

His albums *Back Home Again* (1974) and *Windsong* (1975) reached No.1. Cashbox Magazine named him No.1 album seller and artist in 1974. The CMA named him Entertainer of the Year in 1975. His numerous tributes and awards include the People's Choice Awards, Poet Laureate of Colorado, Record World's Top Male Recording Artist, ASCAP Award for Top Album of the Year, the AGVA Singing Star of the Year, and the Emmy in 1975 and 1976.

His television appearances began in Great Britain in the spring of 1972. John was a guest on the Tom Paxton's "In Concert" show. Denver came across as friendly and likable and Jerry Weintraub, John's manager, saw the dollar signs immediately. Denver was tapped to be the host of a new show on NBC back in the states called "The Midnight Special" which would air right after Johnny Carson's "The Tonight Show." Coincidentally, John was to be a guest for the first time on Johnny Carson and he appeared along with Cheech and Chong, Mama Cass Elliott, Linda Ronstadt, Helen Reddy and Mary Travers (of Peter, Paul and Mary). The ratings were fantastic and Denver was on his way to television stardom.

Back in England, Denver was asked to host a live six-week stint of variety shows. Not only did he sing, he danced, told stories, and acted as host and comedian. These one-hour specials earned spectacular ratings and Jerry built this newfound clout to further bolster John's career. In June 1973, John did his first of many substitute guest stints on the "Tonight Show" and signed a long-term deal with ABC for specials on his own. In November of 1973, Jerry got John on the Bob Hope Show. Bob donned a Dutch-boy wig and Levis and carried a guitar as a parody of John. The appearance made his face and his work instantly familiar to millions of viewers and new fans.

He appeared regularly on television headlining at least one television special a year from 1974 to 1981 and performing with Julie Andrews, Beverly Sills and the Muppets.

In 1977, John had his screen debut in "Oh, God" with George Burns. He starred in the Hallmark Hall of Fame TV special, "Foxfire," with Jessica Tandy and Hume Cronyn in 1987 and was the host of the Grammy Awards in 1978, 1979, and 1982. One of my favorite John Denver performances was in the 1988 TV movie, "Higher Ground," in which he played an Alaskan bush pilot, a role he was perfect for.

Other television appearances included roles on "McCloud," "Owen Marshall" and he was the host of his own 60-minute variety show, "The John Denver Show" in March 1974. His Christmas special, "John Denver and the Muppets: A Christmas Together", is considered a classic.

During the 1980's and '90's John continued to perform and record while devoting himself to various causes close to his heart: conserving wildlife, and the environment, alleviating hunger, curtailing nuclear power and exploring space.

His 1981 album, *Some Days Are Diamonds*, was his last gold album. What many people didn't realize that while the singer had disappeared from the radio and singles charts, he quietly built, through personal appearances, a huge worldwide fan base that was enthusiastic in an almost cult-like sense.

In 1982, on their 15th wedding anniversary, Annie asked for a divorce. After a year and a half separation, their divorce was final on Oct. 31, 1983. John had met Annie in 1966 and had written "Annie's Song" in 1974. "Annie's Song" was one of many songs inspired by their relationship. Eventually, the healing began for their relationship and they remained good friends and devoted parents to Zak and Anna Kate.

In 1984, he wrote a song for the Winter Olympics, "The Gold and Beyond", and performed it at the games in Sarajevo. He published an in-depth and informative autobiography, *Take Me Home,* in 1994. During his career, he wrote more than 200 songs.

On two wintry nights in 1995 John taped (for video and CD release) an extraordinary, 30-song, "Wildlife Concert" to help support the Wildlife Conservation Society at the Sony studios in New York. His remarkable virtuosity was on full display, as he combined talents with some legendary musicians including regular band members James Burton-guitar, Jim Horn-sax, Michito Sanchez-drums, Jerry Scheff-bass, and Glen Hardin-piano.

His last major pop hit was "Perhaps Love" a 1981 duet with Placido Domingo. He continued to make albums and perform and appeared almost yearly in Christmas specials and celebrity golf tournaments. His last television appearance was a beautiful and haunting *Back To Nature Special*—"John Denver—Let This Be a Voice", filmed in the wilds of Alaska one month before his death; he wrote his last song while filming this program on location. John's original recording of "Yellowstone, Coming Home" accompanying this footage is wonderful.

His last public performance was in Corpus Christi, Texas on October 5, 1997. John lived to see his new *Best of John Denver Live* put him on the Billboard chart for the first time in years and shortly before his death, John received an offer from a major record label.

He won a Grammy in 1998 (posthumously) for *All Aboard,* the Best Musical Album for Children and was inducted into The Songwriters Hall of Fame in 1999.

Chapter Eight—John Denver— Humanitarian, Environmentalist and World Citizen

John Denver's music always reflected his concern for the improvement of the quality of life for all people—environmentally, socially, and politically. He was asked to serve as a member of the President's Commission on World and Domestic Hunger. He was one of the five founders of the Hunger Project, and, as part of his commitment to UNICEF he was a member of the fact-finding delegation, which toured African countries devastated by drought and starvation.

He was awarded the Presidential "World Without Hunger" Award. He was a true international presence dedicated to world peace and the elimination of hunger. He was a supporter of the National Wildlife Federation, Save the Children, The Cousteau Society, Friends of the Earth and The Human/Dolphin Foundation. He created "Plant-It 2000, a plan that urged people all over the world to plant as many trees as possible by Year 2000— over 100,000 were planted world-wide in its first year of operation.

He was a board member of the National Space Institute, and in 1985 he received a medal for public service from NASA. (This honor was usually reserved for space flight designers and engineers.) John Denver's interest and commitment to the space program was enormous. In preparation for the possibility of going into space, John passed the NASA physical examination to determine physical and mental fitness needed for travel and also flew and landed the Space Shuttle simulator. He was

Master of Ceremonies at the Goddard Dinner, in Washington, D.C. and was a speaker at the Werner Von Braun Dinner at Marshall Space Center.

His concert tours reached millions globally, from the U.S. and Canada, to Australia and New Zealand, the Orient, and the U.K. He was much admired in Ireland, Holland, Germany, France and Italy.

In the 1980's and 1990's, John's travels crossed ideological lines as well. In 1984 and 1985, John Denver was one of the first Western artists to tour the Soviet Union following a resumption of cultural exchanges with the U.S. He returned to the U.S.S.R. in 1987 to do a benefit concert for the victims of Chernobyl. Denver was the first artist from the West to do a multi-city tour of Mainland China, in October of 1992.

"My music and all my work stem from the conviction that people everywhere are intrinsically the same," he said. "when I write a song, I want to take the personal experience or observation that inspired it and express it in as universal a way as possible. I'm a global citizen. I've created that for myself, and I don't want to step away from it. I want to work in whatever I do—my music, my writing, my performing, my commitments, my home and personal life—in a way that is directed towards a world in balance, a world that creates a better quality of life for all people."

In 1976, John Denver co-founded the Windstar Foundation, a non-profit environmental education and research center that works towards a sustainable future for the world.

As a committed citizen working for the improvement of the quality of life for all people, John's 25th album, *One World*, featured the internationally acclaimed single, "Let Us Begin (What Are We Making Weapons For?)." A separate and unique version of the song was recorded in Moscow as a duet with the well-known Soviet singer Alexandre Gradsky. That recording was the first time a Soviet artist was allowed to perform on a record with a major American singer. The powerful video, "Let Us Begin," moved viewers around the world.

In the summer of 1993, John Denver was the recipient of the prestigious Albert Schweitzer Music Award, given to him "for a life's work dedicated to music and devoted to humanity."

Close friends say that when asked why he spent so much time overseas, visiting ravaged areas of the world, trying to focus attention on serious problems—in recent years his attention was on the orphans from war-torn areas—his answer was "I have to do this." And, yes, his "missionary-like" involvement in overseas concerns probably took its toll on his marriages and his career.

John had a way of just showing up for life and it was rarely a career-based decision. Whether it was a village in Africa, a lake with great fly-fishing, a golf course, a friend's birthday party, an Orioles game, an Oshkosh air show, John felt and acted on his commitment to the human race, to his family, his friends, his fans and to the planet.

A 2-hour special on A&E Television, The Wildlife Concert, first aired in 1995. A longtime conservation enthusiast, John performed this concert in celebration of the 100th Anniversary of the Wildlife Conservation Society. The WCS, headquartered at the Bronx Zoo in New York City, is one of the largest conservation organizations in the world, and John served on its Board of Directors.

The concert is available through Sony/Legacy on a 2-CD/s-Cassette audio release including 29 songs, and through Sony Music Video as a 113-minute home video including exclusive-to-video footage. "The Wildlife Concert" portrayed John in a variety of musical backdrops including solo, full band and string quartet accompaniment. The setting is live and intimate, and captured the essence of the artist, as his millions of fans adored him across the world. Included in this riveting performance were John's best-known hits, several brand-new songs and some very special surprise selections, many of which were captured live for the first time ever.

"We wanted to call this the Wildlife Concert, most specifically out of our relationship with The Wildlife Conservation Society and their support of this project. And, to really underline more than I think the body of music does, to raise people's consciousness and the awareness of wildlife, of wilderness, and how much it has to do with our lives; how much a part of our lives it is...Although I've been aware of the Wildlife Conservation Society for a long, long time, I'm not sure that a lot of other people are so aware. I think they're doing more hands-on work then anybody else in the whole environmental or conservation movement...we invited our fan clubs from all over the world. We had people from Europe, from Germany, from Holland, from Texas. They were all outside singing 'Country Roads' I heard at one point, but it was very, very cold out there, and they were waiting to come in, and started singing this song. I can't tell you what that means to me to know that people all over the world know my songs...

It's a real diverse collection of music. It doesn't all fit the theme, but hopefully it opens the door, or the ear, in a way that people will connect with that we're here about. It's not so much what we're saying in each of these songs, it's what we're here for. And, hopefully that comes through in all of the music.

I'm really grateful to all of the people who've been a part of making this happen. It's an opportunity that's come forward in a very strong way that I haven't had for a large number of years. And, it's been a great frustration in my life, and I really am grateful and glad that I had the opportunity to do a show like this. And I hope that it gives me the opportunity to do a lot more music for people. To keep singing, to keep doing the work that I have the opportunity to be a part of for the environment, for the Wildlife Conservation Society, and other environmental organizations. And, it feels like a wonderful new beginning, and I'm very, very excited about that."

Chapter Nine—The Music

The music of John Denver has been described as a cross between contemporary folk, country and pop: a joyous celebration of nature, love and the simple pleasures of rural living. John characterized his style as "coming out of folk music more than anything else." As to how he created his music he was quoted saying, "Usually an idea that feels like a song that you can make a whole thought out of...when I have a chance to build on it I do. Sometimes it takes months. Sometimes a song comes on and it takes over and I know that I better get out of the way and not do anything."

"As a kid I was really shy. I spent a lot of time either outdoors or alone with my guitar. The outdoors was my first and truest best friend. Whether it was in the desert in Arizona when I was in grade school, or wheat harvest in Oklahoma, or later working in the lumber camps in the Pacific Northwest, nature has always felt like my best friend. And because of that, when I began to try to express myself, it was a perfectly natural thing to use images from nature. I think that is one of the things that allows the songs to reach so many people all over the world."

"My perfect song is 'Rocky Mountain High.' I couldn't change one word or note of it to make it better. It says exactly what I want it to say." John also was quoted as saying, "The *best* song I've ever written is 'Poems, Prayers & Promises'. That song is my best statement. I couldn't have said in a more concise manner exactly where I stand in my life today."

"What I sing about is what I know. That's where the music comes from. I'm not trying to make life anything it isn't. What I'm trying to communicate what is so about my life. What I feel. Every once in a while, you realize what is so for you. You need to look inside yourself. When you find out what your truth is, you are on top of life. The truth is not what you see. The truth is what you think about what you see…I used to wonder how I would feel about working, going on tour, after achieving everything that was really important to me. And I've found that more than anything else I want to share this joy in my life because I see an absence of it everywhere else."

John had always wanted to do a duet with Olivia Newton-John. He had written "Fly Away" after a romantic experience that made him feel like he wanted to just "drift away." He played it for Olivia who loved the song and she did the back-ups for it; it is a beautiful and haunting single.

"My Sweet Lady" was written by John for Frank Sinatra who was looking for songs by contemporary young writers. Frank liked the song and recorded it in 1971.

John wrote many songs for many people. And, of course, John wrote a number of songs for Annie, "Annie's Song" being the most famous. He also wrote "Follow Me," which is on his second album, *Take Me To Tomorrow*, for Annie. "When we were first married, I couldn't afford to take her with me on tour with the Mitchell Trio. At times she couldn't understand why I had to leave and I couldn't blame her for feeling that way." Both Mary Travers and June Carter Cash also recorded "Follow Me" later. Another song that he wrote for Annie was "Goodbye Again." This song was the third song in the trilogy of "Jet Plane," "Follow Me" and "Goodbye Again." John said about these three songs, "They're all about leaving someone you love for whatever reason. I think each song is a little bit older…I don't think I'm a very mature person sometimes. But I do think the songs are maturing. "Goodbye Again" appears on the platinum-selling album, *Rocky Mountain High*.

"Rocky Mountain High" took about nine months to write. "I had the chorus to it that I had gotten from a camping trip to Williams Lake, about 25 miles from Aspen. I was telling these guys about this meteor shower. I said, you guys are gonna see some shooting stars tonight and you're not going to believe it. So it's gettin' dark and I noticed, there was no moon that night, and we were up at about 11,000 feet and there are so many stars and the sky gets to be so deep and so clear that you have a little pool of shadows from the starlight. And then these guys were saying, all right, shooting stars…and then pretty soon there were balls of fire going across. It goes all the way across the sky, you can see the smoke, you can see it and you can hear it. It's great, it's so far out, and I was saying, Rocky Mountain high, I've seen a ray of fire in the sky and the shadow of the starlight, look at that. And then it took me awhile to write that song, to put the story around that song, which is totally autobiographical. Then "Annie's Song" I wrote in about 10 minutes on a ski lift. See…the songs, they come when they come and I can't force them and it's not my objective to do that…"

"Like a Sad Song," was yet another song written about being apart from Annie. John wrote this song in Perth, Australia—he had just won the CMA Entertainer of the Year Award as well as Song of the Year for "Back Home Again." As he sat all alone with his victories in his hotel room, he missed the closeness of Annie and was moved to write the song.

"How Can I Leave You Again" was written on a plane from Aspen to Los Angeles while John was filming "Oh, God!" with George Burns. Although working on the film was very exciting, John would have to commute back and forth to Aspen on weekends to see Annie, Zak and Anna Kate. The song was inspired by his misery at having to leave his family at the end of every weekend.

John wrote "Back Home Again," from the album of the same name, after having been on the road for what seemed like forever. Not thrilled with the constant packing and unpacking, he was sitting in his loft at home "debriefing" with himself, while Annie was downstairs cooking, and got inspired to write the song.

"Autograph" was written in 1980 in the desert at Lake Powell. Lake Powell is the largest man-made lake in the states and is a recreational paradise. House boating is the big pastime on this lake surrounded by miles of deserted beautiful rock canyons. The song sprung from his distaste for signing autographs. John preferred that his lasting signature for fans to be his music.

John Sommers wrote "Thank God I'm a Country Boy" and it was to become one of John's all-time biggest hits. It was also the theme song of the baseball team, the Baltimore Orioles. John was a frequent guest at the games. "He [John Sommers] was a banjo and fiddle player with a group called Liberty. They played in Aspen, and I remember the first time I heard the song I thought, 'That's the perfect song for me. I was gonna write that song, doggone it.' It evokes everything I felt about visiting the farm my father was raised on with 11 other kids. We were simple, hard-working folks, leading a simple life not found in any city anywhere. I signed Liberty to my own record label and took them on the road as my opening act. I would do my show, then I'd get them back up and we'd do 'Thank God I'm a Country Boy'. When I started clapping my hands to get the audience into it, the place went crazy. It was like that every time we performed the song."

"Dancing with the Mountains," believe it or not, came from exposure to the disco scene that was so big in the 70's and early 80's. John noticed that people escaped by going into clubs and dancing all night. It became like a medication. When you are dancing in the mountains, you are ski-ing, he reasoned. Dancing with the ocean, you are surfing or sailing. It was one of his favorite songs. "Downhill Stuff" was written after John had taken a very long hike that seemingly was all uphill. You start to think about the downhill that is still to come. He wrote the song in about an hour.

One song (of a few) to come out of John's EST experience was "Farewell Andromeda (Welcome to My Morning)." Andromeda is the name of a galaxy and the picture of it is on the inside of the album, *Farewell Andromeda*. Andromeda is the name John gave to whatever you have blamed before you began to take responsibility for your own life. From the same album is "I'd Rather Be a Cowboy." John wrote this song out of his conflict of being happy in the mountains and having to go back to the city to sing.

"The Eagle and the Hawk," from the 1971 *Aerie* album, arose from a documentary John did with Robert Reeger and Morley Nelson. Morley, an expert on birds of prey, made it a practice to bring injured birds in and help them heal so that they could go back to the wild. The show was going to document the story of one of these birds. "I had a great experience," John said. "To walk to the top of a hill at sunset and let a young golden eagle go. He had been injured, had his wing repaired over a couple of months, and we were gonna capture it on film right at sunset, as you see on the album cover. Eagles are the symbol of so many nations. Standing there with that eagle on my arm, I got a sense of why they represent so much power, strength and wisdom. And there was the song."

In 1981, John wrote the song, "Perhaps Love" for operatic tenor Placido Domingo to sing on an album that marked the tenor's first attempt at pop singing. Denver joined him in singing the song on the *Perhaps Love* album. "Domingo's a wonderful man, a warm, generous and wonderful human being," said John. "It was incredible working with him."

His album, *It's About Time*, is dedicated to his father, Lt. Col. (Ret.) H.J. "Dutch" Deutschendorf, with whom he had established a closer relationship in later years. He died in 1982.

After being separated from Annie for several months in 1982, John was traveling in China by himself, his first stop being Shanghai. It was the morning of June 10 in Shanghai and the evening of June 9 in Colorado where Annie was. It was their anniversary. John called her and got her at home. They had laughed over the fact that they were both looking at the same moon. The conversation had brought them closer, at least temporarily. Out of that experience, John wrote "Shanghai Breezes."

"World Game" on *It's About Time*, Denver said, "is out of a concept of Buckminster Fuller's describing what we're trying to learn how to play if we're going to survive." The title song, he said, "is how I feel part of the human family...We have to start living that way. Life has always been about survival, you or me, and when it gets down to it, me first.

Throughout history change in society has generally come out of revolution and violence. I don't negate history but we live in a new world now. There are new options. Now, if this is the last barrel of oil, I have a better chance of surviving by sharing it with you than trying to keep it from you. Now, peace is a conscious choice. I have great confidence in people to make a choice when the options are clear…Part of what I'm doing through my music is putting the new options out there."

John wrote "African Sunrise" during a visit to the village Burkina Faso in Africa. He was on a fact-finding mission for the Hunger Project delegation from the Carter Administration. This was a trip that, while disheartening for John to see the malnutrition and starvation up close, he became more resolved in his commitment to be a part of eliminating hunger in the world.

"The Gift You Are" is a beautiful song John wrote for his new baby, Jesse Belle. I play this song often for my rebirthing groups, leaving nary a dry eye in the house. It is deep, healing, and a gift for everyone.

John loved Alaska. The songs he wrote about Alaska include: "Alaska and Me" and "Higher Ground" (co-written with Joe Henry and also the theme from his TV Movie by the same name) from the album *Higher Ground;* "To the Wild Country" from the albums *I Want to Live* and *Earth Songs;* "Whalebones and Crosses"," American Child", and" Wrangle Mountain Song" from the album *Autograph.*

Chapter Ten—The Tributes

Thank God He Was a Country Boy—by Gene Weed, 1997

As you get older one of the things you like the least is seeing the names of people you respected, admired and loved appearing on the list of people who are no longer with us. I guess most of us expect and accept it as part of life. In the past couple of years we've said goodbye to some truly wonderful country music entertainers. It is never easy to say goodbye because it registers an end to a relationship we've treasured. Early in October we had to say goodbye to one of our most gifted and giving artists, John Denver.

What made it so painful is that we were forced to say goodbye to him long before we should have even had to consider the possibility. The tragic plane crash that claimed John's life in the waters off the northern California coast took from us a still young and vibrant creator and performer of the music we all love.

John never apologized for being country; he sang it proudly all over the world. "Thank God I'm a Country Boy" was his theme song, and his recording of "Country Roads" inspired the opening production number of several of the Academy of Country Music Awards programs. He won our awards and captured our hearts. We will all remember him because his music will be there for us.

We need also to remember him as the man who helped the world wake up to conservation and recycling; the singer who stopped on his way to a concert to clean up trash along the highway; the tousled hair musician who came to Los Angeles to sing at a L.I.F.E. (Love Is Feeding Everyone) concert because people needed food. I don't recall John ever saying "no" to a call asking for his help for a good cause. I will remember John Denver for his unselfish respect for other artists.

I recall a night at the Universal Amphitheatre when he and I were standing backstage watching Gary Morris perform. You could see the admiration in John's eyes as he listened to Gary hit notes no earthling was supposed to reach. Halfway through Gary's moving rendition of "Wind Beneath My Wings" John turned and looked at me and said, "You know, God blessed every one of us appearing on this stage tonight with the ability to sing…he just blessed Gary a little more." Thanks, John, you've left us with a legacy of songs and memories we will enjoy forever.

*   *   *

A sublimely sentimental, reflective and sometimes brooding man with a true poet's soul, John Denver possessed keen sensitivity to the world around him, and an uncanny ability to capture layers of emotion in words and music. His sincerity was such that he was one of the only songwriters who could get away with a line like "You fill up my senses…Like a sleepy blue ocean, like mountains in springtime, like a walk in the rain…" and not sound sappy…An underrated singer, he had a clear, perfect-pitch tenor that could soar like the mountains, was sometimes gentle, often high-spirited, always deeply intuitive. *Midwest Today*

He performed in the world's leading concert halls and sports arenas and in the remotest African villages. His partners on stage and in the recording studio ranged from Kermit the Frog and the Muppets to opera tenor Placido Domingo and classical violinist Itzhak Perlman. During his career, he sold more than 100 million albums. *Bart Barnes/Washington Post, Oct. 14, 1997*

John Denver was a dedicated champion of the environment…his soaring music evoked the grandeur of our landscape and the simple warmth of human love…he opened many doors to understanding among nations. *President Bill Clinton*

*   *   *

In concert, John Denver was a masterful showman. Usually he never left the stage for over two hours, even when his band took a break, and he sang his heart out. Playing 6 and 12 string guitars, electric guitar, fiddle, mandolin, and piano, Denver took his listeners to all of those magical place he had taken them before—from the "Country Roads" of West Virginia to the "Rocky Mountain High" beauty of Colorado to the "Country Boy in Paris" and to the high seas on the "Calypso". Denver even took them to China, where a month-long visit inspired his hit single, "Shanghai Breezes."

It could truly be said that as he got older, he got better. Last year when he played the Rosemont theater, the Chicago Sun-Times said he "delivered" a powerful performance filled with sweet surprises—renditions that were truer and richer than when he first performed them…"

A fan that attended a Sept. 20 show in Baltimore, wrote shortly before John was killed: "By the end of the concert he was absolutely glowing! I can't remember seeing a person look so happy…except maybe if I'd looked in a mirror at that moment! The concert was such a gift."

*   *   *

There's nothing like a John Denver concert for cleansing mind and soul. "It's always high quality," described singer-guitarist Denny Brooks, one of Denver's long-time musicians. "Sometimes, it's magically great. But it's always great."

*   *   *

Dear Jeannie,

Thank you for a great read. Your love really shines through making the story special. My "John Denver story"—when Tony (my youngest) left for college I had a major "empty nest syndrome." He was only going to the University of Hawaii from Maui but it seemed like he was gone forever. The first day I cried *all* day and listened to his John Denver album (I'm not sure which one) all day. It sounds silly but John Denver helped me cry and also helped me stop.

Love, Louise

            *   *   *

Today, John Denver is more than a performer and singer/songwriter. He's an American icon. The mere mention of his name evokes an immediate image even among those few who are not familiar with his music. Regardless of ethnic heritage, generation, race, or social class; in Hong Kong or on the streets of New York City, most of us think we know who John Denver is. In Manhattan, the cabbies still beep their horns, "Hey, J.D.!"

To understand why is perhaps to understand ourselves. Maybe it's the idealism or his signature optimism—that sense of hope that is so American—today, so easily scorned; given short shrift in these cynical times. Nevertheless, it is that part of the unique American character that is so admired by people around the world. How else can one explain the monumental and enduring global popularity of songs like "Take Me Home, Country Roads" and "Annie's Song" today in Russia and even Patagonia.

But to know John is to listen to his songs. It is in the music that he's most at home, most himself.

There was a special magic within the hallways and inside the mixing and editing rooms at Sony Music Studios that cold week in February; but especially so on the main soundstage where the warmth shared between John and the audience was memorable. Those of us lucky enough to be there will never forget. Fortunately, I think we've captured it here. Take a moment and listen. You will be surprised. The Wildlife Concert is the music of John Denver. An American voice. A wandering soul—

Maxim Langstaff, April 1995, NYC

            *   *   *

It was revealing that this man—so public, so well known—was not merely generous with his money and his time, but was generous in the most praiseworthy fashion. He gave without needing to call attention to his generosity, to himself...for many people all around the world, millions of people, John Denver's gift was his music. Those clear, touching songs that spoke of the beauty of nature and of simple, deep human emotions. People were touched by his music, people were changed.

John Denver found ways to give to people other than the fans who flocked to his concerts and other than the friends who stuck by his side. He found ways to give to people of his adopted hometown, Aspen, and the entire community that surrounds it...John Denver's concerts at the annual Deaf Camp Picnic—benefits for the Aspen Camp School for the Deaf— were the stuff of legend. Year after year, he would sing to help raise money for programs for children who would never hear his music. And the Deaf Camp Picnics were not his only benefit concerts in this valley. In fact, he played so often, for so many different group and causes, that even those who knew him best and knew him longest can only shrug their shoulders, list a few and then say, "You couldn't keep track. There were so many."

Even though he was giving very publicly, even if he was standing onstage, when John Denver gave benefit concerts in the Roaring Fork Valley, he was standing on very small stages, in front of crowds that were small by comparison with tens of thousands who thronged to hear him play elsewhere. *Andy Stone, The Aspen Times*

*   *   *

We'd get letters from people who had little kids dying of cancer. And John would just sit down by the phone, with a pile of those letters, and make all those calls, one right after another. He'd talk to all those kids and do his best to cheer them up, to make them feel a little better. It was just something he wanted to do. To help. *Carrie Click*

*   *   *

In the end, Annie Denver said it best—as perhaps one would have expected from the woman who knew him best: "He wrote very simple, beautiful songs and he was a complex man." Indeed, John Denver was not—could not have been—the simple, smiling man he appeared to be for so many years. That simplicity that he showed to the world could not have contained the depth of talent that gave voice to the songs he created.

Certainly, that cheerful smile was a true part of his character—for just as it took more than that simplicity to create his music, so to the music required that the simplicity not be a lie. His music could not have reached out to so many, could not have touched so many so deeply if there was a lie at the very heart of it. John Denver was a complex man, both simple and deep. This much we can be certain of.

To much of the world, John Denver was a star. To millions he was a hero, an idol. To Aspen, he was many things. Here, at home, he was much more real. Here, he was a man, flesh and blood—to some, a friend; to many, an acquaintance...here, his virtues were more real. He played and sang at local clubs and benefit concerts, for mere handfuls of people—not the tens of thousand who filled concert halls around the world. Here, his generosity was very real, his gifts touched the lives of people we all knew. Here, too, his failings and shortcomings were more evident. No one is perfect. Some here resented the attention he focused on Aspen during his glory years. And when in darker times, his troubles overwhelmed him, his mistakes were writ large in this small town....John Denver was an artist and, in the end, what an artist leaves behind is his art. Not the scandals, not the gossip, not the success, not the madness. Just the art. And his art—yes, even for those who found it too simple, too naive—had the undeniable ring of truth... *The Aspen Times*

Chapter Eleven—Jeannie's Favorites

"Follow Me" from *Take Me To Tomorrow* (1970)

"Poems, Prayers & Promises," "Take Me Home, Country Roads" from *Poems, Prayers & Promises* (1971)

"Rocky Mountain High" from *Rocky Mountain High* (1972)

"Starwood in Aspen" from *Aerie* (1972)

"Annie's Song"," Back Home Again"," This Old Guitar," "Thank God I'm a Country Boy" from *Back Home Again* (1974)

"Looking For Space," "Calypso" from *Windsong* (1975)

"How Can I Leave You Again," "I Want To Live", "It Amazes Me" (written for the Presidential Commission on World and Domestic Hunger) from *I Want To Live* (1977)

"Heart To Heart," "Perhaps Love," "Seasons of the Heart," "What One Man Can Do" (written about R. Buckminster Fuller) from *Seasons of the Heart* (1982)

"Falling Out of Love," "Wild Montana Skies," "On the Wings of a Dream," "Hold On Tightly" from *It's About Time* (1983)

"One World," "I Remember You" from *One World* (1986)

"For You," "Higher Ground" from *Higher Ground* (1989)

"The Gift You Are" from *The Flower that Shattered the Stone* (1990)

Chapter Twelve—Spirits and Spirituality

Other than the fact that John Denver was extraordinarily gifted, talented, intelligent, wealthy and famous, we did share a few things in common. We both liked flying, we both explored new avenues of spirituality, and we both moved around a lot when we were children. Another thing we shared was our attraction to alcohol. Just making this statement gives me the feeling I'm walking on thin ice.

I know a little something about alcoholism. Actually, I don't claim to be an expert on alcohol abuse or even that I have the right opinions about it. It's a loaded (no pun intended) subject. What I do know is that I drank a lot when I was in my twenties and it seemed to catch up with me in my forties. I walked into an AA meeting a few years ago and stuck around for four and a half years. I was basically drinking three beers an evening but I *needed* to have them. The only time I didn't drink was when I was feeling relaxed—like being on vacation in Hawaii, doing a rebirthing training in Mt. Shasta, or after getting a massage. Otherwise, it seemed like I always felt tense. My three beers helped my tenseness but I was clearly using alcohol to relax.

For the most part, AA was a grand experience for me. I gave up drinking, felt the support of being able to go to a meeting practically anytime of the day or night, and I appreciated the spiritual aspects of "the program." Sometimes it's a truly wonderful experience, to share in a group, or to be moved by another's story.

There were just a few things about the program that bothered me. But, from the AA program's point of view, the things that bothered me were just my "alcoholic self" trying to take my power back from God (or my Higher Power). Surrender was the key, even though some of what was repeated, day after day, month after month, year after year, never felt quite right.

First, there was the "us" and "them" way of looking at the world. The normies "out there" were okay; we were the alcoholics "in here" who had to guard each moment because this cunning, baffling and powerful disease was going to rear up and kick our buts if we didn't watch out.

"Normies" could have a drink or two at a party. We, the alcoholics, could never, ever consider it. I—er, my alcoholic self—didn't like being cordoned off like I had some kind of communicable disease.

The second thing I didn't like was the general belief that if you "slipped" one day and had a drink, oh my god, were you in trouble! That one drink would lead to a second, a third, a fourth and so on and you would most likely die. For me, even before AA, I rarely drank more than enough to cause me to get drunk and/or out-of-control. However, I did drink until I felt good.

And, finally, I was bothered by the fact that "we alcoholics were all the same." We were people with gaping character defects that we had to spend the rest of our lives examining and apologizing for. (Excuse me, I had been raised Catholic—I had enough guilt and remorse to last a lifetime!)

Although I had come to believe—and still do—that a power greater than myself—will restore me to sanity (if I go nuts), I had also come to believe that there are many kinds of alcoholics—not one kind being "better or worse" than the other but a distinction to be made, nonetheless. It appears that there are people who drink who literally cannot stop once they start. A remarkable personality change that you simply can't miss takes over the individual almost immediately after the first drink.

I used to see this on long flights with Pan Am. Passengers would saunter back into the galley, glass in hand—that continued to need refilling—and talk my ear off drunkenly for hours until they would crawl back to their seats and pass out. The next morning, they would wake up and not remember a thing. If one of these individuals drinks too much, he or she can have a "black out" and can do dangerous things to himself or herself or others. But you sure don't need to be in a "black out" to kill someone with your car. Any alcohol can impair your driving. Driving in a "black out" is a guaranteed accident.

John Denver appears to have had a struggle with alcohol given the news items that inevitably were published for all to see when he acquired not one, but two separate D.U.I.'s. One night in 1993, police who determined that he was driving his yellow Porsche under the influence of alcohol stopped John near his Aspen mansion. His license was suspended after he pleaded guilty to "driving while impaired." He performed community service as part of his sentence. But exactly a year later on August 21, 1994, he totaled his Porsche on his way home in Aspen. He suffered only minor injuries and in July of 1996 escaped serious charges when a trial resulted in a hung jury. "Both incidents, said Denver, "were a real wake-up call. It's been a catalyst for taking a good hard look at myself, who I am and who I want to be."

I watched both his first wife, Annie, as well as Dennis Weaver state on television specials about John after his death that he was "an alcoholic." News items after his death often referred to his alcoholic tendencies. It was even hinted that drinking was involved in his accident. One thing I have to say about good pilots—and John was the best—they never take off with alcohol in their system. Never.

Being an alcoholic is not something one sets out to do. I don't think John said to himself when he was 25, 'I think I'm going to write hit songs that come from my heart and oh, yeah, I'm also going to get addicted to alcohol and it's going to cause me some problems.'

I'm not sure alcoholism is a disease either—which is a popular—and medically supported—belief. It is definitely an allergy of some sort. Perhaps we alcoholics are really aliens who landed on the wrong planet. The planet where alcohol is our kryptonite.

In any event, walking into an AA meeting may or may not have been something John did. No one walks into an AA meeting for the first time feeling particularly good about the fact that they can't seem to stop drinking. Alcoholism is still a gigantic stigma in this country (even with Betty Ford and all) and that fact alone keeps many people in the closet about it.

One thing I can say for sure is he drank—we all drank—in Sydney when we were together. But no one got drunk. And my girlfriend Debi, who stayed in touch with John for many years after, said she never saw him drinking. Whatever. Thank God his driving incidents did not involve other people.

I am ever vigilant about drinking. One thing they say in AA, which I tend to believe, is that AA sort of spoils drinking forever. It takes the fun out of it once you become educated about all of the problems associated with it.

John Denver was a very spiritual man, as evidenced by his music and his life. He explored many different aspects of spirituality throughout his life and he was a student of *The Course in Miracles*. This is a self-study program for personal and spiritual transformation that empathizes the necessity of relying on our own internal teacher for guidance rather than looking for teachers outside ourselves. It consists of a text, which sets forth the concepts on which its thought system is based; a workbook for students containing 365 lessons (one for each day of the year), designed for practical application of the course's principles to daily life; and a manual for teachers written in question and answer form to clarify terms and issues related to the course. The course is a spiritual teaching, not a religion.

I became acquainted with *The Course in Miracles* many years ago and I admit I had major difficulty just reading the text. Thankfully, Marianne Williamson and Sondra Ray came along to help interpret the messages the books were here to deliver. Marianne's lectures and her first book, *A Return To Love*, were invaluable resources for me and also for thousands of others who were fortunate enough to be open for this interpretation. Sondra Ray's book, *Drinking the Divine*, is a great examination of the course as well.

"These books have been invaluable to me. " John stated. "Not only in understanding myself but also in organizing and articulating my thoughts about life and the world we live in to others...*A Course in Miracles* tells us that 'you cannot change your mind by changing your behavior...but you *can* change your mind.' And when someone truly changes his mind 'he has changed the most powerful device that was ever given him for change.'

Our world is one of conflict and separation. It is a world of judgment and punishment where others are responsible for our problems. It is an unstable world. As we learn about guilt and fear, and the power they exercise in our lives and relationships, their effect on society and the world as a whole becomes clear. As we begin to understand the power of love and forgiveness, it becomes easier and easier to choose the environment in which we wish to exist. By making the conscious choice, we find that the space in which we live is different; we begin to experience the peace of mind and fullness of heart that is the gift of a loving God."

I'm not sure what shape I'd be in today—or even if I would be alive—were it not for my experiences with rebirthing. John explored many things but I'm not sure if he ever found rebirthing. Rebirthing is a simple yet powerful breathing process that one does for an hour or so that literally renews an individual—spiritually, physically, emotionally and mentally. Many people find that they feel "re-born" after rebirthing. I have used rebirthing as one of my most important tools to reduce stress, let go of past issues, release anger, sadness, and pain. But, most of all, begin anew. Many of us hang on to "stuff" all the way back to birth that can hurt our bodies and our spirits. This is one awesome way to let go. It's like a burden is lifted from your shoulders. One feels a great sense of relief and peacefulness from rebirthing.

I found rebirthing after searching for a long time for some kind of healing from an impossibly awful and frightening childhood. In regular therapy, I was disturbed by therapists' reaction of dismay and horror when I told them about my background after that had insisted that I talk about it. What I loved about rebirthing, when I finally discovered it, was that it was my own journey of healing. No one was saying, "Oh, that's terrible" or "You're going to need at least 5 years of intensive therapy for that one." Instead, I was "getting over" big stuff with amazing rapidity. And people in the rebirthing community were the most nonjudgmental people I'd ever met. Rebirthers never fed the fire of your past "story." They only saw each individual as a perfect being. What a lovely thing.

John had also studied the works of John Bradshaw (*Healing the Shame that Binds You, Creating Love,* etc.) and Marjorie Paul (*Healing Your Aloneness*) and had worked with the most gifted shamans and healers. He never seemed to give up the search on how to make his life a more meaningful one. I wonder if John was aware of the timeless spiritual healing power his own music gave and continues to give millions of people around the world.

"Music does bring people together; it allows us to experience the same emotions. People everywhere are the same in heart and spirit. No matter what language we speak, what color we are, the form of our politics or the expression of our love and our faith, music proves: we are the same." *John Denver*

Appendix I—The Albums

Rhymes & Reasons—1969

The Love of Common People, Catch Another Butterfly, Daydream, The Ballad of Spiro Agnew, Circus, When I'm Sixty-Four, The Ballad of Richard Nixon, Rhymes and Reasons, Yellow Cat, Leaving on a Jet Plane, (You Dun Stomped) My Heart, My Old Man, I Wish I Knew How It Would Feel to Be Free, Today Is the First Day of the Rest of My Life

Take Me to Tomorrow—1970

Take Me To Tomorrow, Isabel, Follow Me, Forest Lawn, Aspenglow, Amsterdam, Anthem-Revelation, Carolina in My Mind, Sticky Summer Weather, Jimmy Newman, Molly

Whose Garden Was This—1970

Tremble If You Must, Sail Away Home, The Night They Drove Old Dixie Down, Mr. Bojangles, I Wish I Could Have Been There (Woodstock), Whose Garden Was This, The Game Is Over, Eleanor Rigby, Old Folks, Medley: Golden Slumbers, Sweet Sweet Life, Tremble If You Must; Jingle Bells

Poems, Prayers & Promises—1971

Poems, Prayers & Promises, Let It Be, My Sweet Lady, Wooden Indian, Junk, Gospel Changes, Take Me Home Country Roads, I Guess He'd Rather Be in Colorado, Sunshine on My Shoulders, Around and Around, Fire and Rain, The Box

Aerie—1972

Starwood in Aspen, Everyday, Casey's Last Ride, City of New Orleans, Friends with You, 60 Second Song for a Bank—May We

Help You Today? Blow Up Your TV, All of My Memories, She Won't Let Me Fly, Readjustment Blues, The Eagle and The Hawk, Tools

Rocky Mountain High—1972

Rocky Mountain High, Mother Nature's Son, Paradise, For Baby (For Bobbie), Darcy Farrow, Prisoners, Goodbye Again, Season Suite: Summer, Fall, Winter, Late Winter, Early Spring (When Everybody Goes to Mexico), Spring

Farewell Andromeda—1973

I'd Rather Be a Cowboy, Berkeley Woman, Please Daddy, Angels from Montgomery, River of Love, Rocky Mountain Suite (Cold Nights in Canada), Whiskey Basin Blues, Sweet Misery, Zachary and Jennifer, We Don't Live Here No More, Farewell Andromeda (Welcome to My Morning)

John Denver's Greatest Hits—1973

Leaving on a Jet Plane, Take Me Home Country Roads, Poems, Prayers & Promises, Rocky Mountain High, For Baby (For Bobbie), Starwood in Aspen, Rhymes & Reasons, Follow Me, Goodbye Again, The Eagle and the Hawk, Sunshine on My Shoulders

Back Home Again—1974

Back Home Again, On the Road, Grandma's Feather Bed, Matthew, Thank God I'm a Country Boy, The Music Is You, Annie's Song, It's Up to You, Cool an' Green an' Shady, Eclipse, Sweet Surrender, This Old Guitar

An Evening with John Denver—1975

The Music is You, Farewell Andromeda (Welcome to My Morning), Mother Nature's Son, Summer, Today, Saturday Night in Toledo Ohio, Matthew, Rocky Mountain Suite (Cold Nights in Canada), Sweet Surrender, Grandma's Feather Bed, Annie's Song, The Eagle and The Hawk, My Sweet Lady, Annie's Other Song,

Boy from the Country, Rhymes & Reasons, Forest Lawn, Pickin' the Sun Down, Thank God I'm a Country Boy, Take Me Home Country Roads, Poems, Prayers & Promises, Rocky Mountain High, This Old Guitar

Windsong—1975

Windsong, Cowboy's Delight, Spirit, Looking for Space, Shipmates and Cheyenne, Late Nite Radio, Love Is Everywhere, Two Shots, I'm Sorry, Calypso, Fly Away, Song of Wyoming

Rocky Mountain Christmas—1975

Rudolph the Red-Nosed Reindeer, Silver Bells, Silent Night, The Christmas Song, Christmas for Cowboys, Please Daddy, Oh Holy Night, What Child is This? Coventry Carol, Away in a Manger, A Baby Just Like You

Spirit—1976

Come And Let Me Look In Your Eyes, Eli's Song, Wrangle Mountain Song, Hitchhiker, In the Grand Way, Polka Dots and Moonbeams, It Makes Me Giggle, Baby You Look Good to Me Tonight, Like A Sad Song, San Antonio Rose, Pegasus, The Wings That Fly Us Home

John Denver's Greatest Hits Volume #2—1977

Annie's Song, Farewell Andromeda (Welcome to My Morning), Fly Away, Like a Sad Song, Looking for Space, Thank God I'm a Country Boy, Grandma's Feather Bed, Back Home Again, I'm Sorry, My Sweet Lady, Calypso, This Old Guitar

I Want to Live—1977

How Can I Leave You Again, Tradewinds, Bet On the Blues, It Amazes Me, To the Wild Country, Ripplin' Waters, Thirsty Boots, Dearest Esmeralda, Singing Skies and Dancing Waters, I Want to Live, Druthers

John Denver—1978

Downhill Stuff, Sweet Melinda, What's on Your Mind, Joseph and Joe, Life Is So Good, Berkeley Woman, Johnny B. Goode, You're So Beautiful, Southwind, Garden Song, Songs of…

A Christmas Together—1979

Twelve Days of Christmas, Have Yourself a Merry Little Christmas, The Peace Carol, Christmas is Coming, A Baby Just Like You, Deck the Halls, When the River Meets the Sea, Little Saint Nick, Noel: Christmas Eve 1913, The Christmas Wish, Medley: "Alfie the Christmas Tree; Carol For a Christmas Tree; It's in Every One of Us, Silent Night, Holy Night, We Wish You a Merry Christmas

Autograph—1980

Dancing with the Mountains, The Mountain Song, How Mountain Girls Can Love, Song for the Life, The Ballad of St. Anne's Reel, In My Heart, Wrangle Mountain Song, Whalebones and Crosses, American Child, You Say that the Battle is Over, Autograph

Some Days Are Diamonds—1981

Some Days Are Diamonds (Some Days Are Stones), Gravel on the Ground, San Francisco Mabel Joy, Sleepin' Alone, Easy on Easy Street, The Cowboy and the Lady, Country Love, Till You Opened My Eyes, Wild Flowers in a Mason Jar, Boy from the Country

Seasons of the Heart—1982

Seasons of the Heart, Opposite Tables, Relatively Speaking, Dreams, Nothing But a Breeze, What One Man Can Do, Shanghai Breezes, Islands, Heart to Heart, Perhaps Love, Children of the Universe

It's About Time—1983

Hold On Tightly, Thought of You, Somethin' About, On the Wings of a Dream, Flight, Falling Out of Love, I Remember Romance, Wild Montana Skies, World Game, It's About Time

Rocky Mountain Holiday—1983—John Denver and the Muppets

Hey Old Pal, Grandma's Feather Bed, She'll Be Comin' Round the Mountain, Catch Another Butterfly, Down by the Old Mill Stream, Durango Mountain Caballero, Gone Fishin', Medley: Tumbling Tumbleweeds; Happy Trails, Poems, Prayers and Promises, Take 'em Away, Going Camping, Home on the Range, No One Like You

John Denver's Greatest Hits Volume #3—1984

How Can I Leave You Again, Some Days Are Diamonds (Some Days Are Stones), Shanghai Breezes, Seasons.of the Heart, Perhaps Love, Love Again, Dancing with the Mountains, Wild Montana Skies, I Want to Live, The Gold and Beyond, Autograph

Dreamland Express—1985

Dreamland Express, Claudette, Gimme Your Love, Got My Heart Set On You, If Ever, The Harder They Fall, Don't Close Your Eyes Tonight, A Wild Heart Looking for Home, I'm in the Mood to be Desired, Trail of Tears, African Sunrise

One World—1986

Love Is the Master, Love Again, I Remember You, Hey There Mr. Lonely Heart, Let Us Begin, Along for the Ride ('56 T-Bird), I Can't Escape, True Love Takes Time, One World, It's a Possibility, Flying for Me

Higher Ground—1988

Higher Ground, Homegrown Tomatoes, Whispering Jesse, Never a Doubt, Deal with the Ladies, Sing Australia, A Country Girl in Paris, For You, All This Joy, Falling Leaves (The Refugees), Bread and Roses, Alaska and Me

Earth Songs—1990

Windsong, Rocky Mountain Suite (Cold Nights in Canada), Rocky Mountain High, Sunshine on My Shoulders, The Eagle and The

Hawk, Eclipse, The Flower That Shattered the Stone, Raven's Child, Children of the Universe, To the Wild Country, American Child, Calypso, Islands, Earth Day Every Day (Celebrate)

The Flower that Shattered the Stone—1990

The Flower that Shattered the Stone, Thanks to You, Postcard from Paris, High Wide and Handsome, Eagles and Horses, A Little Further North, Raven's Child, Ancient Rhymes, The Gift You Are, I Watch You Sleeping, Stonehaven Sunset, The Flower that Shattered the Stone (Reprise)

Christmas Like a Lullaby—1990

Christmas, Like a Lullaby, The First Noel, Away in a Manger, The Children of Bethlehem, Jingle Bells, White Christmas, Marvelous Toy, Blue Christmas, Rudolph the Red-Nosed Reindeer, Little Drummer Boy, Mary's Little Boy Child, The Christmas Song, Have Yourself a Merry Little Christmas

Different Directions—1991

Potter's Wheel, Ponies, The Foxfire Suite: Spring is Alive; You Are…; Whisper the Wind; Spring is Alive (Reprise), Chained to the Wheel, Two Different Directions, Hold On to Me, the Chosen Ones, Amazon (Let This Be a Voice), Tenderly Calling

The Wildlife Concert—1995

Rocky Mountain High, Rhymes and Reasons, Country Roads, Back Home Again, I Guess He'd Rather Be In Colorado, Matthew, Sunshine On My Shoulders, You Say the Battle is Over, Eagles and Horses, Darcy Farrow, Whispering Jesse, Me and My Uncle, Wild Montana Skies, Medley: Leaving on a Jet Plane/Goodbye Again, Bet on the Blues, The Harder They Fall, Shanghai Breezes, Fly Away, A Song For all Lovers, Dreamland Express, For You, Is it Love? Falling

Out of Love, Annie's Song, Poems, Prayers & Promises, Calypso, Amazon, This Old Guitar

The Very Best of John Denver—1995

Disc One—Annie's Song, Leaving on a Jet Plane, Goodbye Again, I'm Sorry, Follow Me, My Sweet Lady, Seasons of the Heart, How Can I Leave You Again, Fly Away, Shanghai Breezes, Dreamland Express, Back Home Again, Poems, Prayers, & Promises, Thank God I'm a Country Boy, Grandma's Feather Bed, Matthew

Disc Two—Rocky Mountain High, Take Me Home Country Roads, Wild Montana Skies, Eclipse, Like a Sad Song, Some Days are Diamonds (Some Days are Stones), Heart to Heart, Sweet Surrender, Looking for Space, Calypso, On the Wings of a Dream, What One Man Can Do, Perhaps Love, Sunshine on my Shoulders

All Aboard—1997

Jenny Dreamed of Trains, Freight Train Boogie/Choo Choo Ch' Boogie, Steel Rails, Waiting for a Train, I've Been Working on the Railroad, On the Atchison Topeka and the Santa Fe, Old Train, Daddy What's a Train? The Little Engine That Could, Last Train Done Gone Down, Last Hobo, People Get Ready, Lining Track, City of New Orleans, Jesse Dreamed of Trains

John Denver: His Greatest Hits and Finest Performances—1997

DISC ONE—JOHN DENVER CLASSICS

Annie's Song

My Sweet Lady

Take Me Home, Country Roads

Sunshine on My Shoulders

What's on Your Mind

I Want to Live

Along for the Ride ('56 T-Bird)

Fly Away

Calypso

Goodbye Again

Some Days Are Diamonds (Some Days Are Stone)

Like a Sad Song

It Amazes Me

Autograph

Shanghai Breezes

I'm Sorry

Perhaps Love

Dreamland Express

It Makes Me Giggle

For Baby (For Bobbie)

Please, Daddy (Don't Get Drunk This Christmas)

DISC TWO—ROCKY MOUNTAIN HIGH

Rocky Mountain High

The Cowboy and the Lady

Christmas for Cowboys

Dancing with the Mountains

Looking for Space

Wild Montana Skies

Downhill Stuff

Farewell Andromeda (Welcome to My Morning)

I'd Rather Be a Cowboy

I REMEMBER YOU:

Baby, You Look good to Me Tonight

How Can I Leave You Again

Sweet Melinda

Everyday
Love Again
Seasons of the Heart
Back Home Again
Follow Me
I Remember You
Friends with You
Leaving on a Jet Plane
DISC 3 JOHN PLAYS FAVORITES
San Francisco Mabel Joy
Whose Garden Was This?
What One Man Can Do
Mr. Bojangles
San Antonio Rose
Fire and Rain
The City of New Orleans
The Night They Drove Old Dixie Down
Let It Be
LIVE...IN CONCERT:
Take Me Home, Country Roads
Today
Surrender
Grandma's Feather Bed
Annie's Song
The Eagle and the Hawk
My Sweet Lady
Thank God I'm a Country Boy
Poems, Prayers and Promises
Rocky Mountain High

Appendix II—Books about John Denver:

Take Me Home—An Autobiography—by John Denver with Andrew Tobier—1994

John Denver's Legacy: A Fire in His Heart & A Light in His Eyes—by Roger Himes—1997

A Tribute to John Denver: Poems, Prayers & Promises—by Javana Richardson—1998

John Denver—the Man and His Music—by Leonore Fleischer—1976

John Denver: Mother Nature's Son—by John Collins—2000

Appendix III—Television Specials and MOW's:

Bighorn—1972

The John Denver Special—1974

A Family Event—1974

An Evening with John Denver—1975

John Denver and Friend (with Frank Sinatra)—1976

The John Denver Show—1976

Rocky Mountain Christmas—1976

Host of the Emmy's—1976

Thank God I'm a Country Boy—1977

John Denver and Friends—1978

Rocky Mountain Reunion—1978

John Denver in Australia—1978

Host of the Grammy's—1978

John Denver in Alaska: The American Child—1978

John Denver and the Ladies—1979

Host of the Grammy's—1980

The Higher We Fly—1980

John Denver and the Muppets: A Christmas Together—1981

John Denver and George Burns: Two of a Kind—1981

Music and the Mountains—1981

Host of the Grammy's—1982

Rocky Mountain Holiday—1984

In Concert at the Met—1984

John Denver's Annual Celebrity Pro/Am Ski Tournament—1984
Leftovers—1986
The Christmas Gift—1986
Foxfire (Hallmark Hall of Fame)—1987
Higher Ground—1988
John Denver's Christmas in Aspen—1988
An Evening at the White House (PBS)—1989
Host of "Christmas in Washington"—1990
The Muppets Celebrate Jim Henson—1990
Montana Christmas Skies—1991

Movies:

Oh, God—1977
Walking Thunder—1993

Videos:

"Let Us Begin (What Are We Making Weapons For?)"—duet with Alexandre Gradsky recorded at Moscow's Melodiya Studios. This was the first time a Soviet and an American artist performed together in a music video.
"Don't Close Your Eyes Tonight"
"Flying For Me"
"Country Girl in Paris"
"High, Wide and Handsome"
"Raven's Child"

Movies and Specials about John Denver:

Take Me Home: The John Denver Story—Movie of the Week on CBS—April, 2000—Starring Chad Lowe, Kristin Davis and Gerald McRaney

VH1—"The Man Behind the Music"—John Denver—October 1998

E! True Hollywood Story—John Denver—October 1998

A&E Biography—John Denver—1997

TNN—The Life & Times of John Denver—1998

Appendix IV—Notable Websites:

www.sky.net/~emily (The Rocky Mountain High Fan Club)

john-denver.org

john-denver.com

johndenver.net

http://legacyrecordings.com/johndenver (Sony Music Site)

impossible-dream.net/john_denver.htm (Starfire's John Denver Memorial Page)

dweller.com/musicofjd.html (The Music of John Denver)

www.btejd.org

austin1.com/jd/Austin

lowellnorman.com

legendsofmusic.com/johndenver

naturemusic.com

Epilogue

On October 12, 1997 John Denver died when the light plane he was piloting crashed into Monterey Bay in California. He was 53. The National Transportation Safety Board concluded on January 26, 1999 that there was too little fuel in one tank of John Denver's Long E-Z experimental aircraft. Regarding the other tank, in an attempt to switch to his back-up tank, John Denver inadvertently put his plane into a roll. The NTSB also blamed the builder's decision to relocate the fuel tank selector handle and an absence of markings on the handle and nearby fuel gauges.

On the day of the crash, Denver and a maintenance technician talked about the inaccessibility of the handle. If the pilot needed to switch fuel tanks, he would have to remove his shoulder harness, turn around, and switch the handle. While doing so, the pilot would press on the plane's right rudder pedal causing the aircraft to roll. Even an experienced pilot would have extreme difficulty attempting this maneuver.

John was a very experienced and highly regarded pilot of many different kinds of aircraft—including (but not limited to) his own Learjet, gliders, single and twin engine aircraft, jets, and acrobatic aircraft—but had only owned this new plane for a few days.

For four weeks following his death, *John Denver's Greatest* Hits remained at #1 on Billboard's Top Country Catalog Albums. I think this would have surprised John—to know how important his music was and continues to be for millions of people around the world.

Afterword

My friend Louise is a very advanced soul. She is a wonderful healer and is a master in the art of reiki, rebirthing and other spiritual processes. After she read my story she theorized that the little green florescent spot—the otherworldly spot that appeared on John's embroidered denim shirt while I was wearing it—signified that my heart chakra was opening (the heart chakra is symbolized by a florescent green color). She surmised that my heart chakra had opened so much that it had actually leaked onto his shirt. That's a wild idea but I wouldn't rule it out.

About the Author

Jeannie St. Marie, a former Pan Am flight attendant and working actress, is a television writer living in Los Angeles.